The Next Marketing Handbook for Independent Schools

EDITED BY RICK COWAN

PROMOTING
INDEPENDENT
EDUCATION
PROJECT

National Association of Independent Schools

75 Federal Street

Boston, Massachusetts 02110

(617) 451-2444

THE PROMOTING INDEPENDENT EDUCATION PROJECT

This handbook is a publication of NAIS's Promoting Independent Education Project (PIE). PIE is a multi-year endeavor intended to promote greater public understanding and appreciation of independent education and to increase the size and diversity of the applicant pool of member schools.

Strategic initiatives to meet PIE's goals focus on: research, training, public relations, networking and consumer products. Our audiences include parents making educational choices, legislators and public officials, those responsible for foundation and corporate giving, and the leaders of the national educational community.

SPECIAL THANKS TO:

— Ramona Ravel Martineau, editorial assistant, for her unflagging effort, endless patience, and unfailing humor.

— The Committee on Boarding Schools, Tom Farmen, chair, for seeing the *Handbook* as a means to its mission.

— Steve Clem, Selby Holmberg, Barbara Stock, John Esty, and Peter Relic, NAIS/PIE colleagues, for institutional support and personal encouragement.

—Marjo Talbott and Carol Cheney, for their groundbreaking work on previous editions.

— Marc Kaufman and Patrick Santana, designers, for turning the editor's vague ideas into an engaging graphic surround.

— Gabriel A. Cooney, for sharing, once again, his evocative photographs.

— Catherine O'Neill, Sally Greene, Kamala Hess, and Julia Small, for their invaluable and ongoing work in promoting and distributing this book.   — *Rick Cowan, Editor*

ISBN 0-934338-75-2

Principal photography by Gabriel Amadeus Cooney

Cover photo courtesy of Northfield Mount Hermon School, Photograph by Lilonel Delevigne.

Design and production by Desktop Publishing & Design, Boston, MA

Printed on recycled paper ♻

Library of Congress Cataloging-in-Publication Data
    The Next marketing handbook for independent schools / edited by
    Rick Cowan. p. cm.
      ISBN 0-934338-75-2 : $22.00
      1. Private schools --United States--Marketing--Handbooks,
      manuals, etc. I. Cowan, Rick.
    LC49.N49 1991
    371'.02'0973--dc20
                                                91--39467
                                                CIP

Contents

INTRODUCTION

How To Succeed in School Marketing Without Really Selling

LEARNING TO FLY WITH THE MIND'S EYE

My hobby is flying an old airplane. My profession is the marketing of independent education. Although it's taken me some years to recognize the connections, flying and marketing have a lot in common. Like marketing, flying is fun, polyphasic (requiring continually divided attention) and at once visual, verbal and quantitative. Both endeavors demand simultaneous big picture vision and micromanagement . . . and both are unforgiving of carelessness and inattention. It's as easy to crash a marketing project as it is a plane, though the consequences are usually less dire.

As a student pilot struggling to master the shifting geometry of a landing pattern, I realized that I was flying the plane inside my head as much as I was flying it through the air. The more successfully I could visualize how my craft was climbing, descending or banking, the better I was able to control it and the smoother the maneuvers became. This "mind flying" also made me a safer pilot. As the control of the plane became more intuitive, I could devote more attention to other crucial cockpit tasks—traffic avoidance, radio communication, navigation, and engine monitoring.

As first steps in learning to "fly" the marketing process at your school, I offer a diagram (fig. A) and an illustration.

LEARNING TO LISTEN WITH THE PAINTED EAR

Veteran marketers know that the process really begins at the bottom of the diagram with monitoring—or in less fancy language, listening. In the largest sense, monitoring is what justifies marketing and distinguishes it from mere selling. The marketer begins with the needs of the consumer while the stereotypical salesperson is focused on her own needs or those of her employer.

By listening carefully and using the knowledge gained to improve our product or service, we mar-

Figure A: Marketing Model

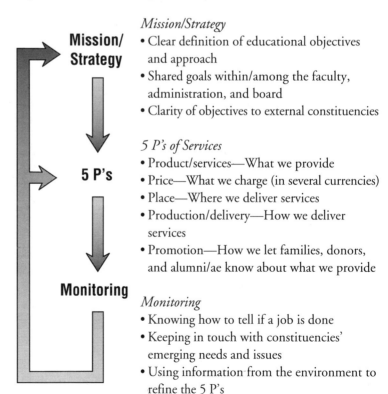

Mission/Strategy
- Clear definition of educational objectives and approach
- Shared goals within/among the faculty, administration, and board
- Clarity of objectives to external constituencies

5 P's of Services
- Product/services—What we provide
- Price—What we charge (in several currencies)
- Place—Where we deliver services
- Production/delivery—How we deliver services
- Promotion—How we let families, donors, and alumni/ae know about what we provide

Monitoring
- Knowing how to tell if a job is done
- Keeping in touch with constituencies' emerging needs and issues
- Using information from the environment to refine the 5 P's

keters justify ourselves and our budgets. The feedback loop in the diagram thus represents marketing's saving grace and perhaps our only defense against critics who deplore the ever-expanding resources capitalism commits to our intangible work. In the 70's and 80's American auto manufacturers learned the hard way that customers must be listened to. Those independent educators who neglect to listen to their students, parents, applicants, donors, and communities in the 90's may find themselves reenacting Detroit's woes of the 80's.

It's as easy to crash a marketing project as it is a plane, though the consequences are usually less dire.

When her 7 year old son ignored her, a friend of mine remarked that she "might as well paint an ear on the wall" as talk to the child. Just as monks in the middle ages kept skulls and other such *memento mori* in their cells to remind them of their mortality, we marketers of independent schools might have ears painted on our office walls to remind us of where our job begins.

It is no coincidence that the theme of listening emerges as the *leitmotiv* of this handbook. Virtually every author suggests ways of monitoring the interests and aspirations of our critical constituencies. Marketing consultant Rick Dalton uses the word "measurement" to encompass the various forms listening can take in the admission, development and head's offices. "Market research," the more common term, frightens independent school types with its suggestion of massive budgets and rows of computers tended by clipboard-toting, white-coated number crunchers. In truth, the planned listening we call market research need be neither expensive nor highly quantitative. Contributor Meg Moulton offers dozens of valuable approaches in her appropriately titled chapter, "The Magic Mirror."

We of your national associations are doing a lot more listening ourselves these days. The extensive market research sponsored by NAIS's Promoting Independent Education effort and SSATB's Market Analysis Profiles program is summarized in the *Handbook*'s final section *(Databank, p.112).*

THE LIMITS OF LISTENING; BEWARE THE "SHOPPING MALL HIGH SCHOOL"

Of all the dangers portended by today's enrollment crunch, none save extinction is more ominous than the possibility of independent schools abandoning their powerful trinity of mission, vision, and tradition. Just as the short sighted pursuit of quarterly profits by American corporations has delivered whole industries to the patient Japanese, pandering to the whims of consumers could undermine our schools.

"You asked for it, you got it!" might work for Toyota, but think of what such total consumer sovereignty would do to our schools. Educational fads shift almost as quickly as hemlines; this year's miracle curriculum is next year's "prescription for failure." If in their zeal to please consumers independent schools come to resemble the "shopping mall high schools" so capably depicted by author Arthur Powell, we will have lost something precious.

THE GOAL OF YOUR ALL-STAR MARKETING TEAM

It's been a pleasure to draft and coach the All-Star Marketing Team whose wisdom you now have at your fingertips. They are an able, articulate and amusing lot who have generously shared their hard-won knowledge. If more of the right students reach the right independent schools in the right quantities as a result of knowledge imparted by this book, we will have partially achieved our goal. If those students are served well by those schools, we will have achieved it entirely.

— *Rick Cowan*
October, 1991

The Next Marketing Handbook for Independent Schools

The Least Theory and Fewest Terms You Need to Know

RICK COWAN

3 KEY CONCEPTS

In thinking back on all the marketing textbooks I've slogged through over the years, I recall only three concepts that have proven to be of daily value. This is not to say that "brand extension" and "channel management" are not important, just that "segment," "position" and "target" are the most immediately useful to those who market independent education.

1) SEGMENT: TO BREAK THE TOTAL MARKET (USUALLY TOO LARGE TO SERVE) INTO SEGMENTS THAT SHARE COMMON PROPERTIES.

Like grain farmers, marketers must sort the wheat from the chaff. For us, the chaff is anyone unlikely to have a need or interest in our product. Since our intangible product is sought by people with children and the children themselves, parenthood is our first distinction. Admission officers who don't keep this distinction in mind make expensive mistakes. No matter how persuasive the brochure, a blanket direct mailing to neighborhoods largely populated by empty nesters, singles and retirees has little chance of success.

You can segment along all sorts of dimensions. Those that have to do with the external facts of people's lives (their zip code, age, income level, marital and/or parental status) are usually referred to as demographic. Those that attempt to distinguish among us by the way we think are often called psychographic. The demographic marketer says that I am likely to behave like the person who lives next door. The psychographic marketer predicts my consumption of goods and services by how I view myself and the world around me. Psychographic researchers come up with delightfully reductionist schemata. In the early 80's Arnold Mitchell of SRI International developed the famous VALS (values and lifestyles) system which divides all humankind or at least all American consumers into 9 groups: survivors, sustainers, belongers, emulators, achievers, "I-am-me'ers," experientials, societally conscious folk, and the "integrateds."

The most effective segmenting comes of coupling demographic and psychographic information. Increasingly powerful computers and compliant credit and governmental agencies have enabled direct marketers to track their quarry via car registrations, credit card transactions, birth records, and membership/donation files.

2) POSITION: TO DETERMINE WHERE YOUR PRODUCT OR SERVICE WILL FIT IN YOUR PROSPECT'S MIND.

Some advertising historians trace this term to the grocer's shelves where packaged goods jockey for prominent position. The word's current usage is metaphorical, suggesting where the product or service exists in the mind of its intended purchaser.

The positioning of one's offering is perhaps the marketer's single most important decision. The object of the game is to find your corner of the consumer's consciousness (sometimes referred to as your "niche") and then exploit it, expand it, and defend it. If you don't bother to position yourself, your customers and competitors will do it for you—but unless you're *very* lucky or have an absolutely bulletproof lock on what you're selling, they won't put you where you want to be. Those who fail to position themselves usually end up misunderstood, unknown or ignored. As management guru Tom Peters remarks, in the competitive marketplace it's "niche or be niched."

The most effective segmenting comes of coupling demographic and psychographic information.

For another perspective on this slippery concept, imagine ladders of awareness in your mind. For most products or services you'll be able to name a few purveyors. For example, if I ask you about insurance companies, you might respond with Prudential, Allstate, Metropolitan Life and The Traveler's. Your relative awareness of those companies' names and services suggests how they have positioned themselves.

The options for entering the market are basically three:

1) Displace someone above you,

2) Relate yourself to someone above you ("7-Up —The UnCola," "Avis is No.2. . . we try harder")

3) Bring in a whole new ladder as did Ted Turner with his revolutionary Cable News Network and Fred Smith with the Federal Express concept of nationwide overnight delivery.

3) TARGET: TO LOCATE AND ADDRESS THE MOST PROMISING MARKET SEGMENT.

Targeting is what happens after you have positioned yourself and segmented your market. Once you know who your intended audience is and what space you intend to occupy in their minds, you can begin to aim your communications.

As promotional media become more and more expensive, marketers (particularly those with small budgets) must forsake wasteful and therefore expensive shotguns in favor of the more efficient rifle. The rise of cable TV and precisely targetable direct mail and the declining influence of broadcast TV and mass market publications are symptoms of how important targeted promotion has become.

Given our traditionally skimpy budgets, we independent school marketers must be especially canny in our targeting. As you evaluate a promotional medium or campaign, keep the initials "CPE" in mind. Cost Per Exposure is how commercial advertisers evaluate the real price tag of a promotional effort. For our purposes*, an exposure could be defined as our message reaching someone who is likely to have the need and ability to "buy" independent education. Although inexpensive in terms of sheer audience reached, a medium with a high percentage of non-parents or parents of non-school age children might well have a prohibitively high CPE for our target market.

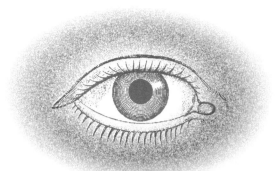

THE MARKETING OF SERVICES: WHEN YOU CAN'T SEE WHAT YOU GET

The distinction between marketing of services and the marketing of goods is one that escapes a lot of otherwise savvy admission officers and school heads. Since most of the marketing we're exposed to is for packaged goods, it's understandable that educators who find themselves with marketing responsibilities conceive of the task in terms of Pepsi vs. Coke or Toyota vs. Ford. Service marketing is a somewhat different beast and one that requires special care and feeding.

ENROLLMENT MARKETING AS A PERFORMING ART

"Goods are produced, services are performed."
—John Rathwell, *Marketing in the Service Sector*

Ponder for a moment the implications of Rathwell's insight. Think of the education your school provides as a "performance" such as a play you might attend at a theatre. The education that you and your colleagues "perform" every day can't be tasted like the Pepsi or driven like the Toyota. It does, however, last for a lifetime and, despite the much publicized successes of the unschooled, education increasingly influences achievement in this, the information age.

Returning to our play, let's determine exactly what you are purchasing when you buy a ticket to a performance of "Six Characters in Search of an Author." I submit that you are purchasing the *promise of satisfaction.* You hope that the play will amuse, entertain and edify you but unless you've already seen it, you can't be sure of that.

What is that family in the admission office waiting area hoping to purchase with their tuition

---

* Different marketing goals obviously require different targeting strategies. Schools seeking socioeconomic and ethnic diversity would define a valid exposure quite differently from those mounting a campaign to yield more full-pay applicants.

dollars? Market research suggests that they are buying the *promise of* achievement, self-esteem, friendship (or social acceptance), plus mastery of the skills needed for future success. Although unlikely to mention it when quizzed on the spot, the more thoughtful parents are also likely to have expectations of moral and intellectual growth. The fact that none of these things can be touched makes many admission folk nervous. In their anxiety they clutch at what can be touched, seen, and shown. Thus is born the most sadly prevalent confusion in independent school marketing, the one that turns hundreds of well-meaning admission folk into real estate salespersons.

MANAGING THE EVIDENCE BY SURROGATE AND METAPHOR

If buyers of intangibles purchase the promise of satisfaction, then our task as the marketers of education is not only to communicate but to document that promise. We must "manage the evidence" even more artfully than those involved with tangible products. Professor Theodore Levitt of the Harvard

You are whom you enroll...

Since student bodies tend to replicate themselves, your current population is the first place to begin in segmenting your market. Although anecdotal information and untested assumptions abound, how much do you *really* know about the families now enrolled at your school? What do they read? What kinds of cars do they drive? Where did they go to school? How do they view your curriculum? What are their political beliefs? Why did they chose your school over public, independent or parochial alternatives?

Oregon Episcopal School asked parents and guardians these questions and many more in a recent survey. See Chapter 9 (p. 57) for the story of this school's innovative approach to targeting its market.

The positioning of schools: beyond the prestige-ometer

In the bad old days, most independent schools were positioned along a very few dimensions. Most of these related in one way or another to social prestige. In recent years many of the 245 boarding schools that my marketing consortium represents have begun to position themselves in more productive ways. Among the factors behind this change are the meritocratic effect of standardized aptitude testing as required by selective colleges, the expanding diversity of America's population, the increasing availability of financial aid, and the growth in the numbers of students who make or heavily influence the decision on where they will go to school.

Although the prestige food chain still dominates the market, thoughtful families and visionary independent educators have begun to carve significant niches out of something more substantial than *The Social Register*. Thus we have schools that position themselves to serve nascent performing or visual artists, competitive skiers, the socially or environmentally conscious, international students or those with different learning styles.

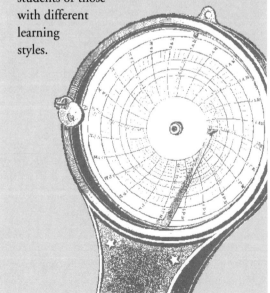

Business School, the West Point of capitalism, suggests that those of us who market services have two basic tools. In *The Marketing Imagination* (MacMillan, 1986), he says that we must rely either on surrogates (previous or present users of the service) or on metaphorical reassurance.

I JUST WANT TO TESTIFY. . .

Those who have experienced the value of any service and are willing to talk to others about it are the most convincing marketers. Testimonials are as effective for your school in the 1990's as they were for St. John in the 6th century. The most successful independent school marketers I know are always figuring out ways to connect satisfied current students and their parents with prospective students and their parents. Testimonials needn't be tacky. As the authors of subsequent chapters illustrate, you should incorporate this approach in everything from catalogs and viewbooks to videos to the design of school tours and training of tour guides. Faculty members, alumni and fellow administrators are also powerful evangelists; let them, too, testify to the quality of your school's education.

METAPHORICAL MARKETING

The challenge of concretizing the intangible is best met metaphorically. Religious marketers have employed this technique brilliantly for centuries. The Bible abounds in metaphor—faith is a mustard seed, righteous behavior is a straight and narrow path, and temptation is a snake. Thinking back to the insurance companies we spoke of earlier, notice that they, too, employ objects to symbolize their service—a pair of protective hands (Allstate), a huge rock (Prudential), and an umbrella (Traveler's).

Another example of the use of metaphor in service marketing is the book-lined, oak-panelled, diploma-laden office favored by expensive attorneys. Such tangible surroundings are intended to impart confidence in the intangible services rendered by those who inhabit them. In just such a manner, the decor of your office, your clothing, and the beauty and condition of your campus are indexes prospective applicants and their families will use to gauge the quality of your school's education. Although such impressions are undoubtedly influential, admission officers who remain "trapped in the tangible" often miss more significant marketing opportunities. (See "The Martian and the Real Estate Person, p. 8.")

RETAINING SERVICE CUSTOMERS

To get customers for intangibles, we must create surrogates or metaphors for tangibility. To *keep* such customers we must regularly remind them of what they're getting. The service customer usually doesn't know what she's getting until she doesn't. Satisfaction is mute; its prior presence is affirmed only by its subsequent absence.

Retention can be a barometer of both your school's health and your marketing ability. A student in hand is worth 6.7 in the bush. Veteran admission officers and heads devote plenty of energy to keeping kids aboard. Beyond what high attrition suggests about families' satisfaction with your school, remember that the work to replace the lost student comes out of your hide. According to recent NAIS statistics, the average independent school must interview nearly 7 students to enroll 1.

NAVIGATING THE ENROLLMENT RIVER

Although virtually every diagram of the enrollment marketing process represents it as a funnel, the image is not quite apt. For one thing, all the water poured into the mouth of a funnel flows out the bottom. Enrollment marketing doesn't and shouldn't work that way. The "leaks" in Don Smith's "Deluxe Funnel" (below) illustrate some of the ways inquirers will leave the enrollment funnel without enrolling at your school.

I would suggest the river as a more accurate metaphor since all the water that flows into a river doesn't make it to the sea. You might think of the 17 authors who follow as seasoned guides, ready with crucial advice as you paddle into the rapids, backwaters, oxbows, floods, marshes, and even pollution of this "enrollment river." *Bon voyage!*

Your Fundamental Funnel

6.7 inquiries
Inquire ⇨ Apply
(conversion)

2.4 applications
Apply ⇨ Accept
(conversion)

1 enrolled student
Accept ⇨ Enroll
(conversion>yield)

* Ratios of Inquiries to Applications to Enrollments for 1989-90 at NAIS's 713 active members

Your Deluxe Funnel*

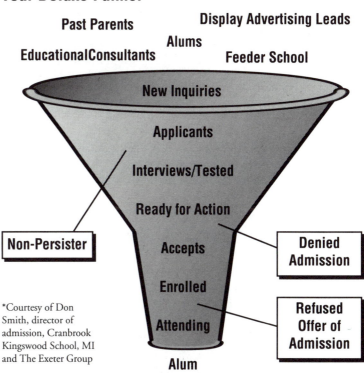

Past Parents
Display Advertising Leads
Alums
EducationalConsultants
Feeder School
New Inquiries
Applicants
Interviews/Tested
Ready for Action
Non-Persister
Accepts
Enrolled
Denied Admission
Attending
Refused Offer of Admission
Alum

*Courtesy of Don Smith, director of admission, Cranbrook Kingswood School, MI and The Exeter Group

Rick Cowan is the director of Boarding Schools, a marketing consortium cosponsored by NAIS and SSATB. A frequent writer and speaker on enrollment marketing, he is the editor of this handbook and a member of the NAIS Promoting Independent Education Task Force. A 1985 Klingenstein Fellow at Columbia University's Teacher's College, Rick began his career at Choate Rosemary Hall (CT) and was subsequently a member of the faculty at The Pingree School (MA).

His interest in non-profit marketing began at the Massachusetts Society for the Prevention of Cruelty to Animals where he served as director of public information and editor of Animals Magazine.

The Martian and the Real Estate Person:
An Exemplary Tale

What exactly are we marketing? Had an observant Martian accompanied me on my visits to hundreds of independent schools over the years, her answer to that question would probably have been "real estate." Like most prospective parents and students, I am usually paraded by or through building upon building—libraries, classrooms, dormitories, labs, gymnasia, arts complexes, recreational centers. On one memorable occasion I stood in a driving rain on the half-poured foundation of a library while a zealous head explained his plans for the building in excruciating detail—right down to the location of the lavatories.

Very occasionally, a head or admission officer with intuitive marketing sense will realize that my understanding of her school's wonderfulness derives more from my interaction with the people I meet than the buildings I walk through. Such was the case on my visit to The Greenwood School in Putney, Vermont. Head Tom Scheidler, a distinguished counseling psychologist, and his wife Andrea founded this boarding school in 1978 to serve 4th to 8th grade boys with learning differences. Although he might not consider himself one, Tom is a master marketer of this invisible thing we call independent education. He is not a real estate salesperson.

After an intentionally brief campus tour and a quick lunch, Tom invited me to spend some time with a few students. I eagerly accepted and soon found myself in his living room with a group of boys who happened to be free that period. Before leaving the room, Tom explained who I was and why I was there. "Mr. Cowan visits lots and lots of schools so he probably won't see much new or different in our classrooms or dormitories. But you guys are what Greenwood is really about. Please introduce yourselves and tell him anything you think he might like to know about the school and your experience here."

40 minutes later I was a Greenwood fan for life. The school's success glowed in the boys' faces and rang in their voices. Their sense of community, achievement and self-discipline dazzled my head while their humor, honesty and high spirits won my heart. Greenwood had made a vast difference in their lives, building skills and confidence that previous schooling had either failed to develop or actively undermined. This was independent education at its most powerful.

As I drove on to my next campus and its inevitable real estate tour, I pondered the paradox that independent education's most underexploited marketing resource is our product itself—the students whom we exist to serve.

—*R.C.*

Confessions of a Reluctant Marketer

BRUCE BUXTON

I found myself studying marketing at the Columbia Business School some years ago in an attempt to expand my experience beyond the sheltered groves of academia. I attended to the various lectures, readings, and guest speakers from New York City's leading profits and nonprofits, and discussed case studies in seminars full of bushy-tailed MBA candidates about to graduate to the real world of "Bisneyland." Alas, my naive self was forced to concede to my cynical twin, Manfred, that his worst suspicions were confirmed in the "real world:" top management, when confronted by ambiguity, becomes frightened and confused. It whistles in the dark. It cries marketing. Consultants, memos, retreats, and charts are weapons of choice. The entrails are stirred, the intangible is quantified, surveys and projections are graphed and bound. General Motors introduces yet another world-beater car.

MARKETING AS MANAGEMENT OR LEADERSHIP?

Columbia taught me that dreamy educators have no monopoly on foolishness. We cannot hope to look to our hardball cousins in the "real world" to solve our marketing problems.

Some observers — friends, I'm afraid, of my evil twin — argue that American managers are so used to short-term management of this or that immediate problem they have lost the time, the method, the confidence to think reflectively and thoroughly through any complex problem. So much of managing is knowing who to call, how to maneuver, when to compromise. Any larger difficulty requiring something more than management (leadership, for instance) gets fobbed off on the task force and the consultant. Because most of a school's long-term difficulties can be framed in marketing terms, and because marketing is a bottomless pit — a thing like thinness and richness, of which you can never have too much — nervous directors find themselves timidly asking for "more, please."

In response a thin gruel is dished up expensively and with relish by the marketing professionals. We are told solemnly about the importance of our logo, and knowing eyebrows are raised and voices hushed as we hear about how to coordinate the look of our admissions packets. Judging from the bland predictability of the pricey material we all receive in the mail, the problems posed by sending out the necessary announcements of ourselves are all solved by the same group of consultants. No ordinary intelligent person could solve marketing problems without their help. We must all be like Oliver Twist, hopefully holding out our bowls.

The marketing issue before us is the issue of taking responsibility for dramatizing our identity.

I think marketing is silly and even damaging when it is guided by professionals from outside playing on the fears and insecurities of the board. As Rick Cowan has observed, "A marketing arms race has emerged: Because one school has a $20,000 four-color viewbook, you've got to have one too. If they have a $45,000 video, you better have one too. And the ante keeps going up. Real foes of marketing fear that things might escalate to the point that an independent school education becomes like a bottle of Chanel #5, with advertising and packaging accounting for more of the price than the perfume itself. Think of what a school could do to benefit its faculty, its programs, its students, its library and laboratories if money were devoted to product rather than promotion!"

The oldest sneer at "market man" that I know of is in The Odyssey, when a disguised Odysseus is accused of being a "tallier of cargoes" and, therefore, unfit for sports and noble pursuits. A long tradition of pseudo-aristocratic disdain for vulgar market man runs through our culture from Homer to E.E. Cummings':

> a salesman is an it
> that stinks excuse me…

I still meet teachers who remark in the tone of an unpleasant discovery about the youthful indiscretions of one's favorite maiden aunt, "your school advertises?"

Yet how often have we been surrounded by groups of teachers at parties or meetings where it seemed that the faculty's main social business was the washing of their school's dirty laundry in public? Don't our faculties understand that as a matter of integrity and enlightened self-interest they have an obligation to market the school they represent?

This mandarin disdain is as foolish and damaging to the schools for which we are responsible as any weakness for salvation by consultant. Perhaps it is less pardonable, given our pretensions to wisdom and the purveyance thereof. And isn't there the slightest hint of a timid admiration for the "captains of industry" that allows us to place so eagerly in real world hands responsibility for this unpleasant, risky, and essential task?

The marketing of television news is an interesting case of shallow marketing, a marketing that is, appropriately, completely in the hands of the professionals because, in fact, there really can be no interference from an identity which demands its own script as it provides its own unique product. The news has no identity. It is the news, and the mass market for which it is packaged is the same for each network.

The networks hire actors who help with marketing the program's image. The image is pitched to the audience the program hopes to attract, and the content of the news is manipulated to attract as many viewers as possible. The consumer reigns.

But we are in a business where the customer is not always right. The integrity of our schools must not be sold out by marketing. And it need not be.

Marketing is something we do all the time as part of our social nature. If we cannot market ourselves effectively, how could we expect others to do it? Or, to recast, if we have a true self, our marketing should in some sense be a natural product of that self. Only the organization that has no shape, no self, no defining significance is in true and desperate need of the marketing group. For in such a case, marketing is pure theatrics, all sound and light, like the portentous music and the pretentious sets of the evening news.

True drama can only proceed from the substantial tension of a real identity. In the case of organizations with such an identity, marketing is not *son et lumière*. It is natural self-dramatization, a product of our everyday social and political business.

The marketing issue before us then is not the superficial and really contemptible business of creating a fake identity. It is the issue of taking responsibility for dramatizing our identity. Responsibility for that kind of marketing cannot be placed in the hands of outsiders for one fundamental reason: the control of an organization's image of itself (and of the image it can then project) is the central business of that organization's management. It cannot be delegated. This is not to say that we never need help from marketing specialists. It is to say that we must look, first, to help ourselves.

Some wag observed recently that if you "talk the talk and walk the walk" long enough you become in danger of "thinking the think." I'd turn that into a circular argument and say that the central issues of leadership, management, and marketing are the same. Leaders think the think, teach people to walk the walk and, soon, more and more people begin to talk the talk and think the think.

THE KEY QUESTION: "WHO ARE YOU?"

Some schools are weak, poor places.

Some schools are pretty good, but there does not seem to be much agreement in the school about **why** the school is good.

Some schools are good, and everyone in the school knows **why** they are good. Only these last schools can practice deep marketing. Only these last schools can hope to achieve **excellence**.

The basic marketing question is: "who are you?" Schools with a unified culture answer that question in a choral, harmonious voice.

Read *In Search of Excellence: Lessons from America's Best Run Companies* by Thomas J. Peters and Robert H. Waterman, Jr. This is a study of America's most successful companies — companies like Procter and Gamble and IBM. The authors say about Procter and Gamble:

> Anyone who has been in brand management at Procter and Gamble sincerely believes that P & G is successful more for its unusual commitment to product quality than for its legendary marketing prowess. One of our favorite images is that of a P & G executive, red in the face, furiously asserting to a class in a Stanford summer executive program that P & G "does too make the best toilet paper on the market, and just because the product is toilet paper, or soap for that matter, doesn't mean that P & G doesn't make it a damn sight better than anyone else." (As in most of the excellent companies, these basic values run deep. P & G once refused to substitute an inferior ingredient in its soap, even though it meant not meeting the Army's pressing needs during the war — the Civil War.)

What Columbia Business School did not teach me: *Learning marketing on the job at Falmouth Academy*

Marketing posed a serious problem at Falmouth Academy when I arrived eight years ago. On my first visit, the negative marketing was so strong, I almost fled. I will only remark on the physical side of that negative marketing. The campus was run down, rusty elementary school on an abandoned Air Force Base. When I arrived in July the school was completely unstaffed, empty, and weedy.

I hired a part-time secretary, began to take inventory, and began to wonder how to convince people to send, at a hefty price, good high school students to a new school in such a location. We had a minimal admissions packet, no school catalog, and no money to print one. The only positive marketing which had attracted me to this school in the first place — its superb faculty — was on vacation.

But we survived, and we survived that summer not because of a new video, a revised logo, clever slogans, or new catalogs. We survived because of constant marketing all that summer by a tireless and well-respected faculty in village stores, filling stations, at the beach, in church.

◆ Without that faculty and without their intuitive understanding of the need to market this school and their new headmaster, we would not have made it. Conventional marketing was almost wholly absent, but something else was there. That something else is a **product** of what I call deep marketing.

◆ Deep marketing **produces** the voice in which a school explains itself to itself. It is the natural voice of the school's culture.

◆ Because Falmouth Academy had a **strong** culture, **created** by the faculty and **controlled** by that faculty, they were able to market the school effectively against all odds.

The two story test

Our schools all have stories to tell. My question is, how many of our stories — our good stories — are really the same story, the mythic story of the good school?

I believe that the purpose of what I call "deep marketing" is to make all the good stories part of the **same** story — to discover in the daily experience of the school a series of images that keep our best goals before us and express our best selves.

I suggest that the test of a successful deep marketing campaign would be to ask every constituent of the school to tell two stories. One story would tell the **worst** thing about the school. The second story would tell the **best** thing about the school. In the school with effective deep marketing in place, all the **bad** stories would be **different, individual, particular**. All the **good** stories would blend to produce a choral voice which sang the guiding myth of the school.

THE POWER OF YOUR SCHOOL'S MYTH

The authors remark on one thing which the successful organizations they studied had in common: these organizations generated stories about themselves — mythic stories — that were passed around within the organization at all levels, like the double story about the executive at Procter and Gamble defending his toilet paper and quality control at P & G during the Civil War. Myths and stories are the stuff of culture. If your myths and stories are the stuff of conversation among the parents' committees, the trustees, the faculty room commandos, and the students themselves, your school culture has found expression.

If the leaders in your school are successful at controlling those myths so that they are positive and affirming and consistent, your school is practicing deep marketing.

JUSTIFYING THE WAYS OF SCHOOLS TO MAN

Marketing, like charity, begins at home. We may employ experts to help guide us through the menus of what's available for how much. Marketing experts, if they are any good, have mastered the conventional wisdom. In a way, that is all they should offer. The original essence of the organization must be grown from within by its managers and leaders. These leaders must make sure that the marketing product answers to what is best in the culture of the school.

Purchased marketing products should conform to the realities of the particular school culture. The marketing product—a catalog, video, logo, or ad—ought to reinforce the stories, the shared sense of self that the school culture has produced. Good marketing becomes deep marketing where it begins to speak in the school's voice.

Because management and marketing are so firmly linked in the organization that practices deep marketing, the school's participation in a specific marketing project can become a part of its in-service training, its reinforcement of its own values.

Consider, for example, a school which puts on an admissions open house and requires all its faculty to attend. Announcements of this event appear in the papers with special emphasis on the personal qualities of that faculty. The faculty are each required to make a three-minute presentation to the assembled guests about their most cherished goals and methods. Among the assembled guests are the other faculty members.

Is this open house really for admissions or is this an in-service? It is both. While the parents are sold on the school because of the qualities they see the faculty demonstrate (poise, a sense of humor, academic knowledge, knowledge of their craft, and great personal charm) the faculty is sold on the importance of collegial respect, the importance of co-operation across departments, the importance of intelligence and compassion in the classroom, and the

Building campfires

How do we nourish and coordinate the positive voices in our school cultures?

First, we need to listen to those voices. If we are interested in **controlling** the voices of our school culture and the culture itself, we need to create occasions in which we **gather** the various constituencies of the school into community, and then identify the songs and stories in which we can believe. Then we need to give everyone a chance to learn the words.

I call such occasions "campfires" because at campfires we sing songs and tell stories. I think most independent schools are good at this, but it is important to recognize these campfires when they occur and to be ready to **use** them — to control them, to **market** them — to define the identity of the school.

Here are some "campfires" at typical independent schools:

- all-school meeting every day
- the school newsletter
- the student handbook
- faculty meetings
- memos to the faculty, to the trustees, and to parents
- athletic banquets
- inscriptions on trophies
- parent-teacher conferences
- progress reports

As you can see from this incomplete list, "campfires" include almost all our common speech. In the school practicing deep marketing, even the dedication to the yearbook should have a familiar sense of being referenced, somehow, to the school culture. A reader should chuckle, "Yup, that's Pinkerton Academy, all right."

Campfire case study

How an unwanted student handbook became a valuable marketing tool

We have a student generated handbook. It is a bit "cute," but that is a function of teenage sensibility. Its authors were teenagers. I don't like handbooks. Our accrediting body asked us to produce one, and a group of students here asked me for one. I refused to produce one, but I told our students that if **they** would like to write one, I would consider editing and publishing the result. I gave the ambitious students my collection of student handbooks from other schools including one I had worked on. I didn't like any of them and told the students that if they really felt the need for this kind of pettifoggery, why didn't they at least try to make the handbook helpful, not just some legalistic list of rules. Assuming I had effectively killed this project, imagine my surprise when a manuscript came across my desk full of information about how to solve problems, where to go for help, and how to organize for school. I made no changes. We had it printed and although we still do not publish a catalog, all our inquiries get this handbook. It is, in my view, an essential part of the Falmouth Academy voice.

importance of the mission of the school. As they give respect to their colleagues they feel respect from their colleagues and the larger audience of outside guests. As they talk the talk they begin to think the think. Voilà, deep marketing! A single sales pitch has turned into a management training school and produced an enthusiastic sales force of teachers.

The message behind our myths will get out — in the words on our athletic awards, in our catalogs, in our ads, and if our myths are sound, the myths will do more than marketing can to justify the ways of schools to man.

Bruce Buxton is in his tenth year as headmaster of Falmouth Academy (MA). His interest in shaping school tone dates to his formative teaching experience at St. Johnsbury Academy (VT) of which he ultimately became associate headmaster. In 1980 he spent a year as a Klingenstein Fellow at Columbia University studying school choice issues.

CHAPTER 3: MORALITY IN MARKETING

"Would You Buy a Used School From This Person?"

RICHARD BARBIERI

A ninth-grade tour guide was leading a prospective student and her family around the campus of Northeast Country Day School. The parents, who were Jewish, raised a question that concerned them beyond the enumeration of facilities and programs: "Is there any antisemitism here at Country Day?" Unfamiliar with the term, but eager to please, the tour guide responded: "Oh sure, NCD is a great school, we've got lots of everything here." This true story illustrates the nature of much unethical marketing in independent schools: we act from love of our school, and we only hurt what we wish to help.

THE UNHOLY TRINITY: EMPTY PROMISES, DENIGRATION OF OTHER SCHOOLS AND HIGH PRESSURE

How do we market unethically? In three ways. First, by promising what we can't deliver. A young woman I know, upon graduation from an independent school, sought to pursue a very special college major, which involved an unusual blend of art and biology. Only three schools in the country offered such a program, and after much deliberation, she chose one. Within a month of arrival, she discovered that the majority of the courses needed for the major were not offered on a regular basis, and that it was impossible to put together enough of them to complete a major within four years. By the next fall she was at another school. Independent schools as well, though not offering majors, sometimes promise courses, tutoring programs, special attention to students at one or the other end of the academic spectrum, extracurricular activities, and facilities which exist more in the hopes and plans of the school than in current reality. A simple caveat may be the best protection here. While schools have frequently been sued for "failure to educate," the only successful actions have been those where a school could clearly be shown to have promised a program or a result and failed to produce it. If for no other reason, we should be wary of promises that we know we can't really keep.

Second, we behave unethically when we denigrate others, whether by outright falsehoods, unfair comparisons, or simply a not-so-subtle put-down about the kind of people who go to a rival school. What is the point, for example, of saying that "Our school's SAT median is eighty points higher than that of the local public school"? This sort of ploy will appeal only to those whose desire for snob appeal is greater than their understanding either of statistics or of the nature of a comprehensive public school. In an era when schools are depending more and more on joint marketing efforts to persuade families of the benefits of an independent school education, such hatchet jobs on the competition are especially reprehensible and even self-destructive.

Among each other the wounds of unethical marketing run deep and last long. We exist as independent schools in an intricate web of inter-relationships among each other, and in a tenuous relationship with the rest of American society. If, as the NAIS Promoting Independent Education Project found, over 60% of respondents don't know enough about us to know what kind of a job we're doing, every mis-step we make echoes in an otherwise silent environment, and the misdeed of a single school can cause all of us to be seen in the same negative light. We need new constituencies to survive, and we must avoid errors that cause us to be mis-seen or to be re-viewed with familiar stereotypes of elitism and snobbery. On the other hand, since we as independent schools offer a range of programs and philosophies and carefully seek the right students for our special missions, working together can enhance all of us, and honest assessments of the differences between schools can help ensure both better public relations and a better fit between schools and families.

Third, we can market unethically without ever telling a lie or maligning a competitor, simply by using tactics that are too high-pressure for the situation or the constituency. We have to remember that we are marketing to the vulnerable: to children unable to draw important distinctions about priorities and values, and to parents whose aspirations and fears for their children make it all too easy for them to succumb to the wrong blandishments. A recent workshop on marketing given by the Independent School Association of Massachusetts (ISAM) admissions officers group chose the playful title "Your Sweatshirt is in the Mail" to kick off a discussion about pressure tactics and hard sell in school marketing. Like the law firms which woo prospective associates with lavish summer stipends and big-city wining and dining, only to drop them with a thud into 80-hour weeks with no time out for a sandwich and a night's sleep once they have signed on, we must be careful not to oversell ourselves.

How do we market unethically? In three ways. First, by promising what we can't deliver.

NEW MARKETS, NEW VULNERABILITIES

We must maintain an especially high standard in our marketing to new constituencies, including people of color and first-timers to the independent school world. Again, the reasons are multiple. First, while all dishonest marketing is wrong, it is especially heinous to mislead those who have previously been deprived of educational opportunities — by our own schools and by our society as a whole — and whose hopes for progress are more urgent and more dependent on the quality of their education than those of the general population. Second, where a group is under-represented, the experiences of a few have even greater repercussions. If thirty members of the country club have children at your school, one or two bad experiences may be outweighed by a predominance of good ones. But if a child from a Boys or Girls Club program, a church congregation, or a new target neighborhood is let down by your school, that will be the only voice heard in the community, and a door may be closed permanently. Finally, we must always be aware that like any limited group, we have our own euphemisms and accepted platitudes, which do little harm to those who can see through them, but which simply cannot in fairness be used on those who are unfamiliar with them.

PREYING ON THE RICH AND THE POOR

Two current practices are especially damaging in our work with new groups. At the upper end of the economic scale, it appears that schools are being approached by individuals seeking remuneration for finding new families, especially from foreign countries. It should be immediately obvious that an educational counselor cannot effectively serve a family by finding the right school for their child while being paid by the school for sending them referrals.

At the other end of the scale is a more common and more cruel practice. All too often independent schools encourage lower-income families, especially those who would diversify the school, to apply, knowing early in the process that aid resources are limited. They then admit the child, but offer no financial aid at all, or a clearly inadequate amount. The result? Dashed hopes for a family wooed and then spurned, and a school which either boasts or laments that it is making a serious effort to enroll a diverse student body, but that it just can't get the kids to come. Of all examples of promising what you can't deliver, this may be both the worst and the most common.

BEWARE THE BOTTOM-LINERS

Why do we market unethically? As I suggested at the beginning, because we love our schools — and because we are afraid. Afraid that others won't see the beauties we see, afraid that the school will not attract enough students, or the best students, afraid for our own professional survival if the numbers aren't right. Such fears are hard to assuage, but we can begin by making sure that the right people are in charge of our marketing.

As Dan Heischman, director of the Council for Religion in Independent Schools, said recently in the pages of Independent School, "We may think we have to attract to development and admission work bottom-line types of people, women and men who do the dirty work of an institution. They need to be determined and aggressive, with a keen business sense and a realistic view of what makes a school work. But our chief marketers must also be those in the school who are most in touch with their own values and with the ideals of the school."

TRANSCENDING PACKAGING AND SEDUCTION

Then we need to have confidence in what we are. Bruce Buxton, in his chapter "Deep Marketing," reminds us that the true stories of a good school will be compelling far beyond any packaged presentation. Proctor Academy (NH) Director of Admission Chuck Will made much the same point in a talk at the NAIS 1990 Annual Conference:

"In the admissions business, it is understood that we get to investigate—in great depth—an applicant. We get to interview, study character, size up potential contribution in the arts and athletics, and measure both achievement and aptitude. Having done this, we render our decision. An offer of admission implies that we are convinced that the match is mutually beneficial, and wholly appropriate.

"In theory, while this is going on, the applicant and family are also investigating—in great depth—alternative educational options. Offered admission, the candidate exercises free choice, and the match is right. When we seduce, we pollute the environment in which this dynamic of mutual choice takes place and the right match is jeopardized.

"How do we promote higher yield ethically, without seduction? Help families choose you for the right reasons. Take off your makeup, stop prepping the tour guides with pat responses, and make your school knowable and known, with clarity, depth, and complete honesty. The right kids will come."

GOLDEN RULES FOR SCHOOLS

Many other chapters in this book contain succinct "How To" lists for various areas of marketing. It's hard to do that for morality in marketing, partly because a list of how-tos can so easily be flipped into a guide for misdeeds. But perhaps a few "Golden Rule" principles may be useful.

First, imagine the Reebok is on the other foot. Is your claim to have an outstanding sports or academic program at least as well founded as you would want a young athlete's or student's claims about their ability to be? Is your assertion of ample availability of financial aid as true as you expect a family's declaration of their need for that aid to be? We hear more and more laments today from schools about families who are not following through on their financial commitments, or who professed to understand and agree with the core values of the school but now are constantly challenging it to change in fundamental ways. If we feel deceived by these families, are we certain we did not contribute to an environment in which we would say anything to get them to come, and they would say anything to get us to let them in?

Better yet, imagine you are speaking to a different audience. One episode of the PBS series "Rumpole of the Bailey" featured a judge who applied a simple test to the insanity defense. Would the defendant have performed the act if a policeman had been at his side? If so, he was insane, and if not, not. Try the same test in your marketing. Would you compare yourself to your rival in the same way if its admissions director were in the room? Would you describe your program in the same words to an incoming gifted student or special needs student if a senior of similar abilities were present? Would you give the same assessment of your school's hospitability to children of color if a current African-American or Hispanic family were beside you? If so, you are marketing ethically.

Why should we worry about unethical marketing? One of the chief drawbacks of unethical marketing is that it simply doesn't work. First, because it's too easy to send back an independent school education. Sure, a false claim may bring a family to a campus for one year, but when you're looking for four, eight, or twelve years of an educational relationship, plus as many of parent giving — and a lifetime of graduate pledges — you can't afford bait-and-switch tactics. Second, because independent schools depend on word of mouth far more than on any other form of advertising, and bad word travels faster than good. Get a reputation for treating families badly, for failing to deliver what you promised, or for unacceptable pressure tactics, and you can expect the world to beat a path from your door.

But more important is the destructive internal effect of unethical marketing. As Robert Sproull said of his role as a trustee of a great university, "my concept of trusteeship is to make Cornell eminently worthy of survival and to assure that she does, in fact, survive." The order of elements is the key: insuring that a school survives is meaningless unless we first remember to make it worthy of surviving.

In his recent book *Managing the Non-Profit Organization*, renowned theorist Peter F. Drucker reminds us of our missions: "The non-profit institution neither supplies goods nor services nor controls. Its product is neither a pair of shoes nor an effective regulation. Its product is a changed human being. The non-profit institutions are human change agents. Their product is a cured patient, a child that learns, a young man or woman grown into a self-respecting adult; a changed human life altogether." Think for a moment about the paradox of producing better human beings through unethical means, and remember that a school is a whole: it cannot be a values-based institution everywhere but in the admissions or public information or development office, just as it cannot preach honor in the classroom and dirty tactics on the playing field. We must be ethical everywhere to be ethical anywhere.

We must maintain an especially high standard in our marketing to new constituencies, including people of color and first-timers to the independent school world.

Richard Barbieri, a former teacher and administrator at Milton Academy (MA), is Executive Director of the Independent School Association of Massachusetts. He is a regular contributor to Independent School and other professional publications and has addressed teachers, heads, trustees, development officers and others at numerous NAIS conferences.

CHAPTER 4: THE MAGIC MIRROR

Putting Market Research to Work for Your School

MEG MILNE MOULTON

LISTENING TO THE RIVER

While magical marketing miracles are in short supply in today's competitive marketplace, market research can provide independent schools with the information and direction from which the "stuff" of marketing miracles is made. Today's most successful independent schools are marked by their ability to understand their distinctive competencies and to have available accurate and timely information on which to ponder old paths as well as new horizons. "Listen to the river and you'll catch a trout," an old Irish proverb reads. In order to survive and prosper in the coming years, independent schools will have to "listen" to their marketplace and study their own reflection if they are to be successful fishermen.

The very essence of a good marketing strategy requires understanding and effecting meaningful exchanges — studying the needs and expectations of student/parent consumers and aligning them with institutional strengths and educational mission. With an emphasis on quality exchanges, independent schools will be able to encourage higher levels of customer satisfaction, institutional loyalty and, ultimately, achieve greater enrollment stability.

MARKET RESEARCH: TWO DEFINITIONS

#1 The process of gathering and analyzing information about your school, your school's market and its competitive position within that market.

#2 "An organized method of finding out what you are going to do when you can't keep on doing what you are doing now."
—Charles F. Kettering

An understanding of the marketing environment in which independent schools exist is an important first step in developing effective marketing strategies. In addition to a growing databank of national demographic information, a number of independent schools and organizations have begun to profile their marketplace and measure general receptivity to and awareness of independent education at different stages along the admissions pathway.

The Promoting Independent Education "Briefings" reproduced in this handbook's final section ("Databank") serve as valuable references to the reader in laying the framework for school-specific research initiatives and marketing strategies.

MOTIVATING MOVEMENT DOWN THE MARKETING FUNNEL

The marketing funnel provides a useful graphic representation of the movement of students toward a school and the process of student/parent choice. At the outside lip of the funnel is the universe of all possible prospective families with children of school age who might consider an independent education. The challenge and the opportunity for a majority of independent schools is to stimulate greater interest in the prospect marketplace (tipping more of these families into the funnel) and then to sustain their interest from the point of inquiry through to enrollment.

Market research can be an extremely helpful tool in profiling families at the different decision junctures. It provides schools with the ability to hold a mirror up to their marketplace and determine which "messages" and communications vehicles are most likely to be effective triggers in prompting and sustaining family interest. In addition, market research can provide schools with an expanded sensitivity to the real and perceived needs of different sets of decision makers: parents and their children, traditional and non-traditional families, those requiring financial assistance and those who can pay full tuitions.

Why Market Research?

- To make information available to your school about its image, market and competitive position.
- To gauge the degree of alignment between impressions of your school and the realities of your community.
- To increase your school's ability to serve its students and to increase student quantity and quality.
- To design effective marketing and communications strategies and target them appropriately.
- To orchestrate a match between your school and the real and perceived needs of prospective families.
- To position your school advantageously against the competition.
- To provide information to direct institutional strategic planning efforts.
- To monitor the continued effectiveness of your school's marketing activities.
- To make optimal use of limited marketing dollars and admissions personnel.

How can independent schools encourage more movement down the marketing funnel? This section will spotlight specific marketing and communication hurdles identified through research which must be acknowledged if we are to be successful in deepening an appreciation of the independent school option. The discussion that follows will center on the attitudes of families at two specific marketing and decision-making junctures: prospect to inquirer and inquirer to applicant. An increase in interest within these two groups is most likely to influence bottom-line enrollments and tuition revenues. Once a family's interest has been firmly established, independent schools appear to be reasonably successful in maintaining a high level of commitment.

National School Enrollment Data

- 46 million elementary/secondary students
- 5.35 million private students
- 361,110 students enrolled in NAIS schools

- ⇨ 6.7% of private students attend NAIS schools
- ⇨ .8% of all students attend NAIS schools
- ⇨ .9 decrease in public school enrollment
- ⇨ .8% growth in NAIS enrollments

KEY MARKETING & DECISION-MAKING JUNCTURES

Stage One	⇨	Prospect to Inquirer
Stage Two	⇨	Inquirer to Applicant
Stage Three	⇨	Accepted Applicant to Enrollee
Stage Four	⇨	Enrollee to Graduate

The Marketing Funnel

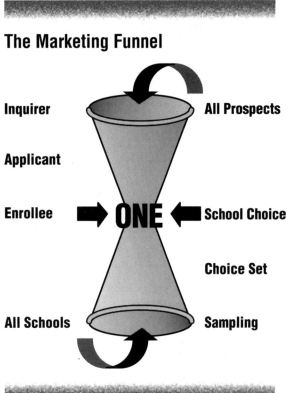

Inquirer

Applicant

Enrollee

All Schools

All Prospects

ONE

School Choice

Choice Set

Sampling

■ STAGE ONE

PROSPECT TO INQUIRER

Nationally, independent schools enroll less than 1% of the school-age population. To increase our share of the market, we must expand the number of families who (for whatever reason) have not previously considered an independent education. Market research can be used as a barometer to test the receptivity of the prospect marketplace and to identify critical marketing and communication hurdles.

RESEARCH FINDINGS INCLUDE

◆ **A quality education surfaces as the single most important school-selection criterion** in the research shared with NAIS. Critical to the marketing success of independent schools will be their ability to "advertise" their educational quality to a broader marketplace. Despite public acknowledgment of educational quality in the private sector, a number of research studies found that little movement toward independent schools can be expected if parents are satisfied with their child's current educational setting.

◆ **Deep-seated loyalty toward and support of the public school exist.** High levels of satisfaction with the public school are recorded in the research. Public schools are viewed as offering a wide spread of extracurriculars, diversity of student types, strong athletic programs and a "real world" setting. Sup-

port for public schools tends to erode toward the middle and high school years along with impressions of their ability to respond to individual student needs and academic potential. Independent schools should seek to market their comparative advantages — such as responsiveness, consistent educational quality, attention to the individual, a committed and competent faculty, small class size, and attention to moral development.

◆ **Non-traditional families (families who have not themselves attended an independent school) dominate the prospect marketplace.** These families appear from the research to have greater difficulty appreciating the value of the independent school experience vis à vis the education offered in public schools. Independent schools will have to articulate more forcefully and precisely their benefits if greater visibility is to be achieved particularly within this family group.

◆ **The word "independent" as a descriptor appears to obscure and confuse prospective families.** "Private," on the other hand, carries with it a tone of elitism, but appears to be a more recognizable adjective. The use of "private" and "independent" together is a possible compromise solution.

◆ **Cost and minimal awareness of financial aid deter many prospective families** from even casually considering an independent school —particularly when compared to the perceived-to-be "no cost" public school. 65% of the prospect families interviewed in one school's research, for instance, were unaware that financial aid possibilities existed. In promoting independent education, financial aid should be given high visibility.

◆ **For those families who can technically afford an independent education, a consumer mentality appears to prevail.** CompAssist calculations currently estimate that incomes of $72,000 for a boarding school and $54,000 for a day school are required to meet tuition expenses. Families with these resources tend to ask, What are the benefits? What is of value? What are the returns on investment? If educational value is not perceived, it is likely that an independent school will have great difficulty stimulating interest in the prospect marketplace and creating the motivation to consider an educational alternative.

◆ **The research reveals a dislocation between impressions of independent school communities and the realities of the actual learning/living experience.** Many prospective families (particularly those personally unfamiliar) view independent schools as elite communities — ones which are removed from

Use and Usefulness of Information Sources

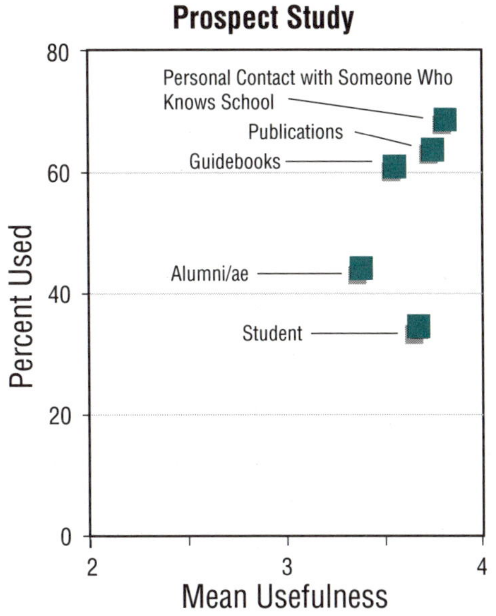
Prospect Study
80
60
40
20
0
Percent Used
Personal Contact with Someone Who Knows School
Publications
Guidebooks
Alumni/ae
Student
2
3
4
Mean Usefulness

the "real world," ones which lack diversity and tend to isolate their students. These perceptions must be erased. In reality, many independent schools are more diverse and more inclusive of different student types than many high-income suburban high schools.

◆ **Word of mouth is the most effective motivator.** While visibility can be gained through advertising and direct mail to the prospect marketplace, positive words-of-mouth (personal references from members within a school's "family") are the most effective way of prompting families from the point of no interest to that of inquiring at an independent school.

◆ **Distance from home, separation from neighborhood friends and transportation all appear to factor into a family's decision to not actively pursue an interest in another educational setting for their child.** To counter these hesitations, transportation links should be considered to ease getting to and from school sites and a school's sense of community and "neighborhood" should be emphasized.

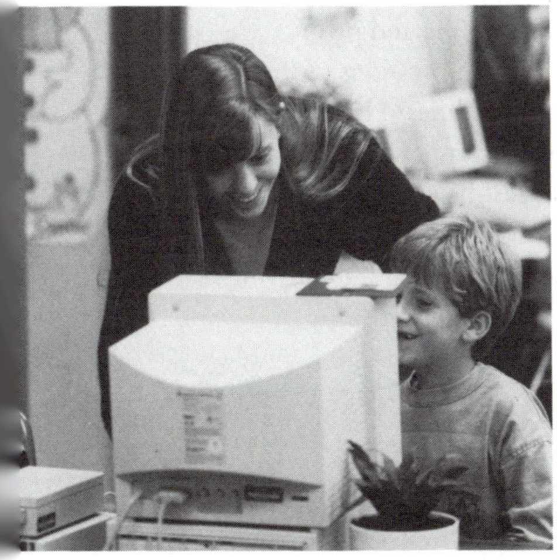

Stage Two

Inquirer to Applicant

Cultivating the potential of a school's inquiry pool requires both sensitivity and persistence. From the point of first contact, the specific information needs of a family must be addressed and a concerted effort must be made to help a family identify those attributes of the educational experience which are valuable and which set the school apart from its competitors (in the public and private sector). Market research has begun to identify those factors which are likely to influence a school's ability to convert its inquiries into applications.

Audiences and Messages

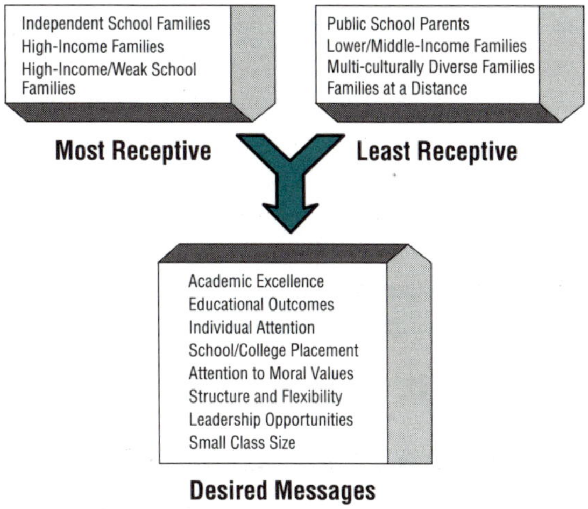
Independent School Families
High-Income Families
High-Income/Weak School Families
Public School Parents
Lower/Middle-Income Families
Multi-culturally Diverse Families
Families at a Distance
Most Receptive
Least Receptive
Academic Excellence
Educational Outcomes
Individual Attention
School/College Placement
Attention to Moral Values
Structure and Flexibility
Leadership Opportunities
Small Class Size
Desired Messages

Research Findings Include

◆ **A private independent education is given high value ratings by inquiring families** in various individual and group market research projects. These impressions of high value do not appear, however, to reflect a concomitant degree of familiarity. Inquiring families would seem to benefit from receiving information and partaking of experiences which will make them more familiar and more able to quantify what they view as "of value." The more a family is able to understand and define for themselves the value of the independent school experience, the more likely they seem to be to make application.

◆ **Inquiring parents with no personal experience with private education represent the majority of families in a school's inquiry pool.** As the research suggests, this parent group is much more likely to focus on tangible outcomes of the independent school experience — evidence of academic accomplishments, breadth of curricular and cocurricular offerings, numbers of computers, the quality and attractiveness of physical setting and facilities, and future school or college placement.

◆ **Non-traditional parents have greater difficulty appreciating the intangible benefits of an independent school community** — the powerful influence of relationships over successful educational outcomes. Illustrating how teachers, students, parents, administrators, and alumni(ae) work together to affect successful educational outcomes will be important to evidence in marketing activities to the inquiring family.

◆ **Inquiring families distinguish themselves in the research from currently enrolled families by their lower median incomes and their greater willingness (and need) to consider financing options** to cover the expenses of an independent school education. More so than almost any other factor appearing in the research, the impact of cost and the availability of financial aid appear to be major deterrents in a family's decision to submit an application. It is critical for this reason that independent schools provide financial planning services and information about financial assistance programs as quickly as possible after interest is expressed.

Financing a Private Education

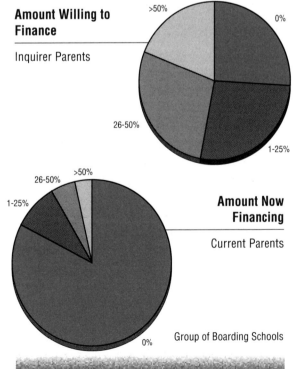

Amount Willing to Finance

Inquirer Parents

>50%

0%

26-50%

1-25%

Amount Now Financing

Current Parents

26-50%

>50%

1-25%

0%

Group of Boarding Schools

◆ **Both parent and child appear to be actively involved in the school-choice process.** The research suggests that targeted marketing strategies should exist which are directed at each of the decision-making partners. To communicate exclusively with just the parent or the child could have a negative impact on a school's ability to increase its inquiry/applicant yield.

◆ **It is personal contact with a member of a school community that appears to most influence a family's decision to inquire and make application.** While families appear to refer to directories, handbooks, videos and catalogs, a school's people network is likely to yield the best return on marketing dollars. Staff time, not money, is required to nurture and organize these programs.

◆ **A campus visit gives families the opportunity to interact with admissions personnel, faculty and students and to observe the "real world" of an independent school.** In the research, the campus visit emerges as one of the most powerful persuaders in a family's decision to apply and later to enroll. Encouraging a campus visit (and return visits) should be a priority activity. Interviews, tours, class visits, parent receptions, special events, symposia, overnights and other prospective family on-campus events should be carefully planned and executed — responding to consumer needs with great attention to detail and putting a school's institutional best foot forward.

■ STAGE THREE

ACCEPTED APPLICANT TO ENROLLEE

Once admitted to a school, a family's final school choice seems to be affected by impressions of value, ability to afford and desire to attend. An understanding of competitive positioning becomes extremely important at this juncture. Who are your school's competitors? To what degree does your school overlap with other public and private schools? What are families' impressions of the quality of your programs and facilities? How to they compare to others in your competitive set? Individual school research must be conducted at this stage to determine how to define your school's niche and how to meaningfully and honestly influence a family's decision to enroll.

■ STAGE FOUR

ENROLLEE TO GRADUATE

Careful monitoring of student enrollments using both quantitative and qualitative research should be in place in order to ensure that satisfac-

The Next Marketing Handbook for Independent Schools

tion levels are high and as many students as possible are being retained for reasons within a school's control. Some student attrition is unavoidable due to family finances and concerns, student discipline problems and academic inadequacies. Exit interviews and surveys of families who decide not to re-enroll should help independent schools answer some of these important questions:

— Why do students leave?
— Do departing students share similar demographic profiles?
— If leaving voluntarily, what reasons are given for not re-enrolling?
— How satisfied are your currently enrolled students, their parents, your faculty?
— Do some grade levels experience greater attrition than others?

RESEARCH ON THE HOME FRONT

"Knowledge is of two kinds. We know a subject ourselves, or we know where we can find information about it."
—Samuel Johnson

How true Samuel Johnson's words ring. A number of sources exist which independent schools can use to find information about their marketplace. The marketing climate described in the preceding pages and helpful other information is distributed by the organizations listed below.

RESOURCES

▧ NAIS PIE Briefings Statistics/Custom Reports Market Research Themes
▧ SSATB MAPS (Market Analysis Profiles)
▧ Center for Education Statistics
▧ U.S. Bureau of the Census
▧ U.S. Department of Commerce

The first kind of knowledge which Samuel Johnson refers to is the subject we know ourselves. This knowledge is close at hand. It is information gained from looking inward, studying your school's own reflection and collecting, organizing and examining financial, admissions and enrollment data.

Successful schools are often characterized by strong and creative leaders who know where to find and how to use information about their school as they set enrollment goals, monitor student flow, plan budgets, measure image, gauge satisfaction levels, target marketing strategies and design commu-

nications pieces. While independent schools are becoming more sophisticated in their ability to collect data, many still struggle with managing and organizing information in such a way that it can be communicated to and used by decision makers.

COLLECTIBLES

Often we hear the words "information is power" or "you can't argue with the facts." Data and information become important change agents in the process of adjusting to external and internal situations. In our information rich society, however, it is important for independent school leaders and managers to be able to have qualified data to use to monitor both positive and negative changes.

Users of information should ask themselves a series of questions:

— WHY do I need the information?
— HOW will the information be used?
— WHAT information is needed?
— WHERE can I access the information?

The marketing manager must have access to hard data — data that records student movement and marketing activity. Essential marketing and enrollment data is profiled on the next page. To whatever extent possible, data should be presented to reflect short- and long-term trends, be kept in a central location and managed by one person. With the relatively inexpensive and sophisticated computer hardware and software available today, the process of gathering, cataloging and computing data is easier, faster and more accurate than ever before.

DO-IT-YOURSELF AND OTHER RESEARCH

A variety of valuable research possibilities exist. They can be either qualitative (based on subjective, non-quantifiable impressions and reactions) or quantitative (resulting in hard data, numbers, percentages) in nature. Market research should provide the accurate and pertinent information school leaders need to map strategy and make decisions. As schools begin to develop a research agenda, the following ten activities associated with a "typical" research project will be important to remember:

The 10 steps of research

(1) Define the research — Why is the information needed? What are the project goals? How will it be used?
(2) Develop a written statement of the research objectives along with a list of the specific

Pieces of the Information Puzzle

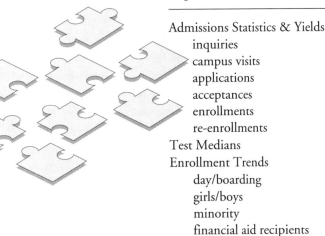

Important data to collect

Admissions Statistics & Yields
    inquiries
    campus visits
    applications
    acceptances
    enrollments
    re-enrollments
Test Medians
Enrollment Trends
    day/boarding
    girls/boys
    minority
    financial aid recipients
    international
Attrition
    school
    division
    class
Information Sources
    phone, letter, current student,
    current parent, alumna/us,
    campus visit, school visit,
    direct mail, advertisement
Feeder Schools
Geographic Distribution
    inquirers
    applicants
    enrollees
Competition
    tuition
    financial aid
    inquiry/application overlap

information that is required in order to meet these goals.

(3) Review existing data to determine if any of the desired information can be gathered elsewhere.

(4) Conduct a value analysis to determine if the value of the information will exceed the cost of getting it.

(5) Design the research project — tasks to be accomplished, individual(s) responsible, timetable, and cost.

(6) Establish a method of collecting the data. If quantitative research is planned, will data be gathered using a mail, telephone or face-to-face survey?

(7) Determine the various research tactics including sampling, instrument design and pretesting.

(8) Supervise and conduct field operations, i.e., implement the survey.

(9) Collect the data and conduct statistical analyses.

(10) Interpret and present the data; extend marketing, planning and enrollment strategies suggested by the research.

The broad outline of these ten steps has been adapted from a list of research steps appearing in Marketing for Public and Non-Public Managers *by Lovelock and Winberg.*

A SAMPLING OF QUALITATIVE RESEARCH POSSIBILITIES

Focus Groups — Focus groups can provide useful forums to listen to the impressions and learn about the mindset of various constituencies, to test new marketing concepts and to set parameters for more sophisticated quantitative research. Ideally groups are limited to 10 – 12 individuals and last for approximately an hour. The conversation is usually led by one individual — working from a set script of issues and ideas. The danger with focus group research often resides in reading too much into the "results" and extrapolating the opinions of a few over too many.

Exit Interviews — If a student decides not to voluntarily re-enroll, an exit interview with the departing student (and, if possible, the parents) can be helpful in researching reasons for leaving. If expectations are not being met and dissatisfaction is present, the school will benefit from knowing about circumstances they might in the future be able to control or alter. Because issues and reasons often fade quickly and response rates tend to be very low, mail surveys of "leave takers" are often not extraordinarily revealing.

Communications Critique — Some research can be relatively informal and spontaneous. One such example is a communications critique. This "research" involves spreading all your school's communications pieces out on a long table.
    What image do they create?
    Is the image positive or negative?
    Is there a family look to your publications?
    Are your various pieces successful in communicating their intended message and the unique qualities of your school?

The Next Marketing Handbook for Independent Schools

How persuasive and easily grasped is your message?
To whom are they sent?
Do audiences overlap? Are messages redundant?

Place your pieces next to your competitors'.
Are distinctives apparent?
Have prospective and current students respond to
your current materials and to those of your
competitors.
What are their reactions?
How would they rate your pieces for design
and content?

*See David Treadwell (Chapter 6) and Carol Cheney
(Chapter 7) for more on publications.*

QUANTITATIVE RESEARCH

A higher level of sophistication is required to conduct quantitative research — research to study in detail institutional image, niche and markets. Extremely insightful market research has been performed (often with professional guidance) on an array of audiences to better understand image, competitive set, factors that influence decision making, demographic profiles of existing and potential markets, used and useful information sources, impact of financial aid, pricing and other marketing issues.

A variety of audiences have been surveyed by independent schools across the country. Among those surveyed have been: prospects, inquirers, inquirers/non-applicants, accepted/non-enrolling applicants, enrolled students, non-reenrolling students, faculty, referral agents and alumni/ae. Research on each of these constituencies could provide significant marketing information.

Sometimes, however, the quality of the information yield is compromised by the lack of clarity and precision in the questions being asked. If your school should elect to do research, each survey question should be carefully scrutinized for its content, wording, sequence and purpose.

Is a specific question necessary?
Are several questions needed instead of one?
Are questions sufficiently specific?
Does the respondent have the necessary information to answer the question? Are questions too sensitive?
Do questions lead a respondent toward a specific answer?

In addition to question content and purpose, question patterns and sequences should be carefully designed to follow in a logical order to encourage participation and accuracy. Pretesting the survey in-strument will help to identify possible survey construction problems.

The three types of quantitative market research used by independent schools include mail, telephone and personal interviews. Each has advantages and disadvantages which relate to duration, cost, implementation, turnaround time, potential biases, and data volume.

QUANTITATIVE RESEARCH

Survey type	Advantages	Disadvantages
Mail	Cost Reply Convenience	Response Time Non-response Bias Follow-Up Mechanics
Telephone	High Completion Rate Spontaneity Survey Duration Minimal Response Bias Sample Size Issue Exploration	Holding Interest Cost Pre-Mailing
Personal Interview	Explanation Issue Exploration	Cost Time Sample Size Possible Bias Response Hesitancy

LISTENING FOR YOUR SCHOOL'S FUTURE

Independent schools exist in a competitive environment. They provide a viable and valuable educational alternative, but one which is not always well understood and appreciated. To survive and prosper in the coming years independent schools will have to be nimble, broadcast their uniqueness and "listen to the river." Market research remains an important "listening" tool with which independent schools can build effective marketing strategies.

Meg Milne Moulton is a principal consultant for Marketing and Enrollment Associates, a firm specializing in marketing and communications for independent schools and their associations. She is executive director of The Coalition of Girls' Schools, a marketing collaborative of girls day and boarding schools and a consultant to the Junior Boarding Schools Association and Boarding Schools. She has formerly served as director of admission at Simmons College. Meg speaks regularly at meetings and workshops sponsored by NAIS, SSATB, and regional associations. Among her many publications are Summary of Market Research Themes, *a report of NAIS's PIE Project.*

CHAPTER 5: ONE TO ONE IS #1
Face-to-Face Marketing

JOY SAWYER MULLIGAN

uring his "interview" for placement in kindergarten, the four-year-old son of one of my colleagues in boarding school admission was asked what his father did for work. No hesitation there: "He talks to people about our neighborhood!" was the sunny, direct response.

At our best and most basic, in day schools and in boarding schools, working with younger students or high school aged boys and girls, that's **exactly** what we in admission offices do. We talk to people—often unconvinced, even skeptical strangers. We give tours, sometimes "once removed" (in print, on videotape, via telephone and letters), sometimes very real. We serve as the first and—at least initially—the primary human link between our educational communities and people who don't know what our schools are all about. It's at once an enormous responsibility and an exhilarating opportunity, captured in an apparently simple gesture: we open the door and invite prospective students and parents in for a look at our "neighborhoods." In fact, though, the gesture is complex. How do we get these people to the door in the first place? What are they coming to see? Is that what we want to show them? How? Are we going to be the sole tour guides or the Pied Pipers of many? How can we AC-centuate the positive and E-liminate the negative perceptions they may secretly harbor about independent schools? (See NAIS PIE "Briefings" in this book's "Databank.") And, finally, how can we make the whole process seem natural and easy, substantial but not overwhelming?

HEART OVER HEAD

Giving commandment status to one definitive rule will guide you as you answer these questions: regardless of what the decision-making balance ultimately is between student and parent, families who sign on our dotted lines do so more from their hearts than from their heads. An admission process that feels comfortable at every juncture—by which I mean one that maintains a consistent tone, that is marked by helpfulness, clarity, unpretentious professionalism, and one that by whatever wizardry makes visible what is invisible (values, standards, academic strength, quality of relationships)—will speak to those hearts. And while creating such a process may begin with us as admission officers, it by no means ends with us. The more enthusiastic voices a family hears, the more "insider guides" a student or parent has, the more perspectives on your school community you can provide, the more at ease a family will feel. Charles Burkett, Vice-President of the Juhl Agency, a marketing communications company in New York, put it this way: "Education… is an intangible. Like a shoe, it must be a good fit. This is an emotional sell, and the comfort level is very important." Effecting that level results in a more productive, meaningful interchange between prospective families and you, from the "Good morning!" they hear when first calling to a "Welcome aboard!" handshake or hug, and at every step in between.

STUDENTS AS HOSTS AND AMBASSADORS

On campus students can be put to use as greeters, tour guides, waiting room hosts, overnight hosts (if you are a boarding school), luncheon hosts, letter writers for special situations, telephone callers. Off campus, armed with information you have provided, they can be ambassadors at their former schools and spokespeople at receptions for prospective families. Where the possibilities for student involvement in admission lie differs from school to school, but however you decide to involve students in your recruitment efforts, remember that an ounce of training is worth a pound of loose buckshot.

Presuming that a "great kid" will, without appropriate direction and aim, give a great tour is dangerous. Even the most carefully selected students (and I would argue for a thoughtfully chosen few rather than an entirely volunteer force) need clarity and focus for this particular task. Early each fall, set aside meeting times for both new and experienced guides: a refresher course for the old hands, and a soup-to-nuts for the new ones. Don't spare details as you define your expectations. Practice shaking hands. Role-play a tour with a frightened, monosyllabic just-barely-thirteen-year-old. Talk about the difference between hiking around with parents and with students. Discuss the tour route or route options. Just before you end the meeting, hand out a booklet (no need to be fancy—merely comprehen-

The multiFACEted school visit: questions to answer before the family arrives

A family is arriving at your campus tomorrow. You have spent countless hours and invested most of your budget in encouraging them to make this appointment. This is not the time to leave the rest of the process to chance. Pondering these questions may help you frame their experience of your school most positively:

- Have you steered the family towards a day and time that shows your school off to best advantage?

- Has the visit been confirmed by card or letter, a map and written directions been provided?

- Does the family know the level of formality at your school and what to wear—a coat and tie or casual pants, a dress or slacks?

- Do they know beforehand how long they can expect to be at your school, whom they will meet and what will take place?

- Once on campus, will they find clearly marked signs directing them at every turn to your office?

- Will students, faculty and staff they pass along the way say "Hello!" and smilingly point the way?

- Will someone—you, another admission officer, a student, a receptionist, a faculty member— greet them at the door by name?

- If they are to go off on a tour right away, will the introductions be made by someone who is confident in that role? If their tour is later, will they be offered refreshment of some sort in something other than a wilting paper cup?

- What is the atmosphere in the waiting room like? Is there a faculty member or student to chat with as the family is waiting for their tour or interview? Or are you—and the admission staff—the only people on campus who know someone this special is here to see the neighborhood?

You know—especially if you've been carrying the weight of all this by yourself—what the answer to that last question should be. Systematically enlisting the cheerful, willing help of people outside your office not only lightens your load, but creates an energy of involvement that, if appreciatively nurtured, will serve your purpose of multi-FACEted marketing for a good long time. Who's to be tapped? Students, faculty members, present and past parents, alumni/ae—a vast multitude at your service, and your school's.

sive) that puts all of this to paper. The following day or days, hoof it out on campus for mock tours, you and experienced guides leading small groups of initiates around the school.

THE MAKING OF A MEMORABLE TOUR

Perhaps above all, discuss ways to make a tour special and memorable, and, at the very least, something more than a canned real estate tour. All tours should not be created equal! For example, you know

The more enthusiastic voices a family hears, the more "insider guides" a student or parent has, the more perspectives on your school community you can provide, the more at ease a family will feel.

from a prospective student's preliminary information card (or a phone conversation, or from a pre-app, or the biographical data on the SSAT score report) that she wants to save all the whales. Make sure that the tour guide knows that instead of looking in on **any** science class, she should steer towards the lab where the marine biology teacher instructs (or otherwise keep her eye peeled for him), make the introduction if they meet, dally longer in the science area, perhaps, cut out some other less important— for this student—part of the tour. As Fred Volkman, Vice Chancellor and Director of Public Relations at Washington University, points out in his renowned CASE lectures, **one-to-one conversation** beats out all other methods of marketing communications. That young girl will remember that meeting with a faculty member or older student who was excited about her particular passion far longer than the fact that she didn't see the radio station. (Unless she's also a fledgling DJ, in which case…) As often as you can manage it, plan one or two such encounters in every tour.

Not all students are good at tours. Some enjoy and are top-flight at making conversation sitting down, cookies and milk in hand; others have been tour guides for two years and would like to try a new role. Enlist these boys and girls in your waiting room to talk with parents and youngsters anxious for the next part of their visit. Schedule them as you would students for tours, or leave their involvement more open-ended: students dropping into your office has real appeal to visitors, and it keeps you connected to the community, as well. Or ask, of your selected group, who would like to host a family for lunch occasionally? Or every Wednesday during the month of January? The more students you can engage in admission activities and the more invested they feel, the more pervasive the admission network becomes. They carry good will even when they're not "on," setting an example for other students who aren't officially (or yet) part of your little army, creating and recreating daily the positive atmosphere you want visitors to witness and absorb as they walk your paths, look into your classrooms, watch a school assembly.

SPREADING THE WORD AND REWARDING YOUR EVANGELISTS

As for off-campus ambassadors, remind all your students, just before vacations, that you've got school brochures (and whatever else you'd like to include) ready and waiting for them to pack into a suitcase or carry home to potentially interested younger friends, friends of friends and third cousins-twice-removed. Encourage (or actually help orchestrate) your present students to visit their former schools and to pass along the good word about your school. If you do arrange these visits through the sending school's counselor or principal, be sure to send along with your ambassador a special note of thanks, including some newsy tidbits on his or her former students, and perhaps even something new from your marketing arsenal—a coffee mug with your school seal, a key ring from your bookstore.

If front-end training and annual re-training is essential for the students whose energy and good

The Next Marketing Handbook for Independent Schools

will you want to harness, doubly so is recognition and recompense. Supporting, nurturing, celebrating students' roles in successful admissions "moments"—these will keep your boys and girls participating enthusiastically. First, keep them informed of their individual impact: share verbal compliments, photocopy notes of thanks or praise you receive from parents who have visited recently, add your own appreciation and brighten up a student's trip to his mailbox. Second, be public and vociferous about their accomplishments; name names. If Drew Jones helped a drop-in family from Nigeria feel as though they'd walked into some educational Shangri-la, say so in a school assembly if you have one, or at least tell his advisor so that mention can be made. Crow in your parents' newsletter about Cindy Casteneda's tireless work as your Head Tour Guide. Third, reward in tangible ways: give a special dinner or dessert for your troops at least once a year, perhaps including a silly or serious "prize" ceremony; send them valentines in February (when tour guides, like many schools, tend to drag a bit); let them know that they're welcome to cookies and a cup of tea in your office whether or not they are scheduled for a tour. In all of this, don't keep your appreciation subtle. Do all you can to keep it both fun and personally rewarding to be a student participant in admissions.

YOUR FACULTY ALLIES

As Steve Clem points out in Chapter 17, the other valuable voices in "talking about the neighborhood" belong to faculty members. How best to involve them? At a faculty meeting early in the year, you might lay the groundwork for their participation by giving a specific example or two of families whose decision to enroll was influenced by a serendipitous interchange with a teacher. (Keep a file on those you hear about from prospective parents and their children.) Combined with your well-timed comments at other meetings throughout the year, this heightens awareness of the importance of everyone's part in the admission effort. Also, offer a menu of faculty volunteer activities: lunch hosts, waiting room hosts, helping with an open house or evening reception, writing a letter or making a call to a particular candidate, or being a part of an "Adopt-an-Applicant" program. Be pleased with one or two volunteers to begin with and, as with your student helpers, be profuse—and specific—in your thanks. Make certain that your school head and dean of faculty know that your colleagues have pitched in and what impact they have had.

PARENTS AND ALUMNI: VITAL VOICES

These adults can also be vital members of your chorus, if chosen carefully and conducted well. As hosts for off-campus admission receptions in their homes, for example, they can talk with both credibility and passion about their children's school and/or alma mater. But whether you put these often eager beavers to work in that particular way, or as telephone callers or letter writers, don't underestimate the importance of firm direction from the get-go: if one of the themes you want underscored is moral values and ethical behavior, arm your helpmeet parents with that knowledge, and talk about examples from their experience that would serve best. Wherever in the admission pipeline you decide to engage these parents (from post-inquiry to post-interview to post-enrollment), be utterly certain that these parents understand the principles Dick Barbieri writes about in Chapter 3 ("The Morality of Marketing"); emphasize especially that denigrating a competitor is foul play of the worst kind. On the more practical side, take a lesson from Proctor Academy's admission office, and provide a sort of parent/alum press kit. Along with a letter explaining what points to cover in conversations with prospective families, they send two current catalogues, a video, and other appropriate printed materials. (You might also share with them some of NAIS's PIE findings, as a motivator and guide for their discussions with prospective parents.) As with both students and faculty, begin with a small force of parents and alums, choosing carefully those people whose voices are varied and trustworthy and whose personalities you can work effectively with.

Your network of fellow marketeers is only as strong as your leadership.

LEADERSHIP AND ENTHUSIASM: THE SINE QUA NONS OF ON-CAMPUS MARKETING

In all of this remember that your network of fellow marketeers is only as strong as your leadership is. Setting an example of apparently indefatigable enthusiasm may be exhausting, but that's what it takes to keep others engaged. It also takes reversing roles occasionally: you have now asked others—students, faculty, parents, alumni/ae—to invest their time and energy in your vision of admissions as a series of personal interactions with individual girls and boys and their mothers and/or fathers. Now and then, give back to that source: volunteer *your* services in areas where your talents lie. Offer to substitute teach a class or two, take over someone's lunchroom duty or study hall proctoring for a day or two, paint a stage set or help get the chorus on stage during their next concert. In short, know and visibly support the other programs on campus. And the fewer official, required duties you have, the more important this involvement is. In such involvement is the foundation for your enlisting others of your community in the hard work, shared responsibility and—when all goes well—tremendous satisfaction of admissions.

In the end, whether your chorus of voices is as big as the Mormon Tabernacle Choir or as small as a barbershop quartet matters little. What matters is that a variety of individuals—you, students living the independent school life, their satisfied parents, happy and productive alums—close the gap between what research reveals most inquiring families *don't* know about neighborhoods like ours and what we all *do* know so well, so specifically, so certainly.

Joy Sawyer Mulligan has served as director of admission and financial aid at The Thacher School (CA) since 1986. Previously, she had taught, coached, advised and done admission work at Governor Dummer Academy (MA), Choate Rosemary Hall (CT) and St. Paul's School (NH). A member of the NAIS Admission Workshop faculty since 1988, Joy has also been a presenter at the SSATB's annual meetings. She has served on the steering committee of the Western Boarding Schools Association and the SSATB annual meeting planning committee. At present, she is a member of the Boarding Schools Committee.

Putting Life Into Admission Publications

LAKE FOREST ACADEMY

You are here.

DAVID R. TREADWELL, JR.

About sixteen years ago, I took my sons David and Jon (then eight and seven) on a weekend camping trip. We headed off to a rather nondescript campground in Maryland with borrowed camping equipment: threadbare sleeping bags, a tent with holes in the top, and a few battered pots and pans.

We did what fathers and sons do on such trips. We skipped rocks, climbed rocks, chased squirrels, and tossed frisbees. Then we fixed dinner, the highlights of which were heaping helpings of Spaghetti-O's and Oreos. (I didn't say we were veteran campers.) Then we repaired to our borrowed tent, the one with the holes in the top.

We lay in our threadbare sleeping bags, I in the middle, and told ghost stories. Then the rains came, first in small droplets, then in torrents. Eventually, the stories ran out, and the rain stopped. It was quiet, and we were drenched. Suddenly, the damp stillness was broken by a question from son Jon. "Dad, why are we doing this?"

WHY ASK "WHY?"

What does a story about an ill-fated, rain-drenched camping trip have to do with an article on admissions publications? Well, my son asked a good question when he asked "Why are we doing this?" The right answers to his right question go well beyond munching Oreos or skipping rocks or ducking raindrops. They revolve around fathers and sons needing to spend time together, even in less than ideal settings.

And now to the central point of this article: if you begin to ask the right questions, the deep questions, in the course of creating your admissions materials, then you almost certainly will end up with better and more effective publications for your school. By "better" and "more effective," I mean publications that have heart, personality, a distinctive flair. I mean publications that live and breathe uniqueness.

TOSS OUT THE GARBAGE

To create publications with heart, you must first toss out the garbage, the piles of preconceptions you may have about "doing catalogues" or "doing viewbooks." You have to deep-six the myths you may have heard such as: "Publications have to be done in-house (or out-of-house);" "A large catalogue is better than a small catalogue (or vice versa);" "Kids don't read (or do read);" or "Red is a better color to use than green;" "Publications should be 'academic' (or flashy);" or… fill in here some preconceptions you may have or have heard.

Too many people charged with developing publications spend too much time too early in the process making decisions that should be postponed until later.

PUT THE HEART BEFORE THE HORSE

In my experience, too many people charged with developing publications spend too much time too early in the process making decisions that should be postponed until later. They decide upon the budget, the design, the outline, the photographer, the size, and the paper stock before they've asked the critical question: "Why are we doing this?" They spend endless hours discussing who will create the publications or who will serve on the review committee or whose feathers can't be ruffled or what special interest group must be appeased. But, alas, they forget to ask "Why?"

PUSHING THE WHYS

Why, then, are you creating admissions publications? To get more students? (Why?) To get better students? (Why?) To get a more diverse mix of students? (Why?) When you keep asking the whys, you begin to get back to the heart of the school, to the central question, "Why does the school exist?" How does it change or improve lives? How is it really different from School X or School Y down the road? What circumstances create the magical moments of growth? Why, in their most honest and open moments, are faculty and students glad to be spending a little time on this particular patch of educational turf? What quirks, large or small, help shape and define the school's personality? Yes, schools do have personalities, though they're often

hard to describe, let alone capture in a printed piece.

SHUT UP AND LISTEN!

To push the whys you have to ask and then listen to the answers. You have to wander around the grounds to see what's really going on, what people are talking about, what they care about. You have to really listen to hear the collective chorus of the school, the song the people are singing. And, when you do, the little quirks, the telling examples, the striking quotes, will begin to emerge that will help later in painting a vivid picture of the place. Talk

Ten Tips on Photography

1. Do use a professional unless you have an amateur at the school blessed with a professional eye.

2. Do have a purpose for each photograph.

3. Try to capture the unusual, but accurately representative, situation as it is taking place.

4. Beware the stock teacher-in-front-of-the-classroom shot.

5. Don't line up a diverse group of students for a posed photograph. Students aren't fooled.

6. Think about the message that the cover photograph conveys. It is the most important shot in the book. (Of course you must first have a good reason for having a photograph on the cover!)

7. Favor action shots over contemplative shots.

8. Ask students — current and prospective — what they would like to see in a school before you go out and hire a photographer.

9. Make sure the photographs illustrate the messages being conveyed in the text.

10. If in doubt, ask, "Why are we doing this?"

with visitors, try to hear and sense what they're thinking and feeling. And, budget permitting, you might even want to conduct some off-campus surveys of prospective students or parents or, even better, alumni. But, if you do off-campus research, which can be very expensive, remember that the goal is to get a better handle on the mindset and heartset of the people being surveyed. It is not to simply "do research." A weighty number-laden report may look good in your bookcase, but it won't do much to inject life into your publications.

SO, WHAT'S THE BIG IDEA?

Once you have done your listening, you're ready to think about the messages you want to convey based upon the listening. You should end up with a BIG message and several smaller supporting messages. There may be some disagreement internally on the message(s), but if the homework has been conducted carefully and the school does stand for something, then disagreements should be kept to a minimum. Not until you have reached this point should you begin to talk about the nuts and bolts of putting a publication together.

THE SEARCH FOR SYNERGY

I've seen time and time again situations where educational institutions treat publications as if they were Mulligan's Stew. A wordsmith whips up a batch of words. A designer concocts some pretty designs. A photographer follows orders: "take pictures of the campus." Each works in isolation. And then someone is instructed to throw it all together, stir and serve. Synergy never enters the picture. Nor do the whys. How does the design work with the words and the photographs? What is the purpose of this or that design — or paragraph or photograph? Do they all work together to support the central message or messages? (Take a look at your current viewbook or catalogue and see the extent to which synergy exists.)

BEWARE THE SMOKE-FILLED ROOM

Sometimes, too many times, the publications process turns into a bloody political battleground. As a result, the song becomes discordant. Or, worse, everyone opts for the politically safe approach. The goal becomes: Let's not offend anyone. And that, experience tells me, leads to turning no one on with your publications. You can't avoid political situations. After all, when you have two or more people in a room you have a political situation. But if you force open and honest discussions at the outset, you

Ten Tips on Writing

1. You do not necessarily need a professional for the writing. You do need someone with professional skills, a feeling for education, and an ability to ferret out and convey the distinctive personality of your school.

2. Remember: less is more when it comes to words.

3. Shun predictable headlines such as "The Students" or "The Faculty" or "The Academic Program."

4. Avoid the ponderous and the weighty — unless, of course, your school is ponderous and weighty.

5. Use interesting examples and telling quotes wherever possible.

6. Imagine you are giving a thoughtful but informal talk to the reader. Then write as you would talk.

7. Pretend the reader is someone whose needs and interests you really care about. (In fact, you better really believe it, not just pretend.)

8. Don't overstate or oversell. It won't work, and it's wrong.

9. Know what you're going to say before you say it.

10. If in doubt, ask, "Why are we doing this?"

can minimize the havoc that political games wreak on the process of creating publications that breathe authenticity and integrity. "But," you protest, "our people can't agree on the messages we should convey!" Then, I answer, you better try to reach agreement. After all, publications should, indeed must, reflect the truth. If the internal players disagree sharply on the whys of the school, then the school has problems that go well beyond publications.

STICK TO YOUR GUTS

The process of creating effective publications can be long and painful. Many times along the way you will be tempted to take short cuts or give in to this or that political whim. Sometimes you do have to take a short cut or give in to a whim. But try at all times to stay focused, to stick to your guts, to keep the whys in mind. Your fortitude will result in a better finished product.

SHUT UP AND LISTEN . . . AGAIN

Once you've completed a publication, especially one that has been done the right way, you will be tempted to sit back, mop your brow, and hope you will never have to endure the same experience again. In fact, if you want to do an even better job the next time around you must re-start the listening process almost immediately. Find out what prospective students (or parents) do or do not like about your publications. Find out whether people both on and off campus believe the publications accurately and interestingly portray the school's strengths and personality. And, of course, monitor the admissions statistics closely for tell-tale signs that the publications are working. You may well need to change the publications the next time, but the principles suggested here should be remembered.

A FINAL WORD OR TWO

We hope this article has given you a better sense of how to inject life and personality into your admissions publications. We hope the question "Why are we doing this?" sticks with you. Doing publications the right way can be difficult, but so is the process of education. In the final analysis, admissions publications should do no more than reflect, in an interesting and truthful manner, the best of the educational process at a particular school. In sum, admissions publications should educate, illuminate, and elevate. Created with an open mind and heart, they can do just that.

David R. Treadwell, Jr., has seven years experience in admission at Bowdoin and Ohio Wesleyan and seventeen years in institutional marketing and communications with Barton-Gillet, Treadwell-Maguire, and Treadwell Associates. He has made scores of presentations at professional conferences and has published articles in popular magazines such as Seventeen *and* Parade *and in professional journals such as* CASE Currents, The Chronicle of Higher Education, *and* The College Board Review. *David holds a B.A. from Bowdoin and an M.B.A. from Harvard Business School.*

Three Case Histories

Three examples of publications developed with David Treadwell's guidelines in mind.

THE CULVER ACADEMY

Culver Academy is a military school in Indiana. Many outsiders assume that because Culver is a military academy it is regimental, strict, and not much fun. They also assume that because Culver is in Indiana it is in the cornfields. In fact, Culver students do have enjoyable experiences; the military characteristics enhance rather than diminish the education students receive. Moreover, Culver is located alongside a beautiful lake. The cover conveys the sense of the campus and also, by showing a crew shell, the emphasis on discipline, but in a positive way. The inside is filled with colorful photos of students enjoying themselves and taking full advantage of Culver's remarkable programmatic offerings and physical facilities.

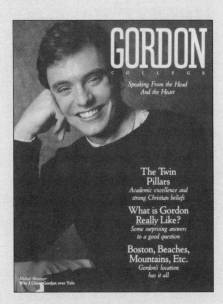

THE PUTNEY SCHOOL

The intent of this catalogue is to convey the overall message: Finding Your Own Voice. It is an appropriate message for Putney, a Vermont boarding school that gives students a considerable amount of freedom and, at the same time, demands that they take individual initiative to find out who they are and what they can be. The cover photograph supports the central theme. The copy inside explains how Putney helps students find their own voices. A subdued yet artistic two-color approach was considered more appropriate than a flashy four-color look. The catalogue was printed on recycled paper. Incidentally, this catalogue was produced in conjunction with a video (created by Warner & Forman). The video and catalogue were distributed together in a compatibly designed box.

GORDON COLLEGE

Although Gordon is a college, not an independent school, the principles discussed in this article still hold. Gordon is one of the top three Christian colleges in the nation from an academic standpoint. The College attracts highly qualified students at least in part because of its Christian emphasis. The theme ("Speaking from the Head and the Heart") conveys the twin emphasis on academic excellence and Christian values. The cover features a student who chose to attend Gordon over Yale University. His reasons support the central theme. The viewbook was developed in a magazine format with each article showcasing one of the major messages.

CHAPTER 7: IN OTHER WORDS
Managing Institutional Identity

A place to prepare,

A time to grow

Discover the boarding school difference...

CAROL CHENEY

Even though I labor in the marketing vineyard every day, I sometimes find myself tangled in its terminology. If the niches and positionings and segments of marketing occasionally stump me, I imagine that the same might hold true for school administrators and trustees who have much more to worry about than this single though crucial aspect of running a school.

Wally Olins' outstanding book *Corporate Identity: Making Business Strategy Visible through Design*[1] has provided me with a fresh point of view and a simple lexicon devoid of mumbo jumbo. Olins' approach might help you, too, understand what you must do to prosper in an increasingly competitive marketplace. In this chapter I have adapted and summarized what I learned from Olins about corporations and added from my own experience in independent school communications.

PURPOSE AND BELONGING, THE ESSENTIAL INGREDIENTS OF IDENTITY

Most successful schools have a clear sense of purpose that is understood and accepted by the entire school family. Understanding and believing in the school's purpose (mission) fosters a strong sense of belonging. Purpose and belonging are the ying and yang of identity, and the identity of the school must be so entrenched that it is evident in all services, behavior and policies.

• The *services* the school performs must project its standards and values.

• The *buildings* and *campus* where the life of the school goes on are compelling manifestations of identity.

1. Some of the ideas and information presented in this article were derived from *Corporate Identity: Making Business Strategy Visible through Design* by Wally Olins, first published by Thames and Hudson in 1989 and currently available from The Harvard Business School Press, Boston. 224 pages with over 350 illustrations, $50.

- The *communication materials,* from alumni bulletins and student recruitment brochures to student handbooks and athletic schedules, must have a consistent quality and character that accurately and honestly reflect the whole institution and its aims.
- How the school *behaves*—to its own faculty, staff and students and everybody with whom it comes in contact, including parents, alumni, suppliers and host communities—is a vital aspect of identity.

WHY SHAPE IDENTITY?

Especially in younger, smaller schools, the management of identity is intuitive, reflecting the founder's or current head's interests and values. In older, larger, more complex schools, the disparate interests of individuals and departments often compete for influence. Unless the school's identity is managed thoughtfully, long term mission and ethos may be engulfed or overshadowed by turf battles.

From the seed of belonging grows the mighty oak we call school spirit. A school will thrive only if its community of people is proud of it and what it does. Its members must share a common culture, agree about what is and is not acceptable behavior within the institution, and totally understand its goals and aspirations.

Very few schools perceive the relationships among the various parts of their identity; very few therefore attempt to control the whole constellation of impressions they make upon their various constituencies by treating everything they do as a part of what Olins calls "a seamless whole." Does your school seek to control its identity, or does it allow factions and indifference to reign? Schools that do not consistently project their identity are vulnerable to incomplete and conflicting images, rumor, myth and lack of visibility.

All other things being equal, schools with good programs and powerful, well-coordinated identities will overshadow their rivals whose programs are just as good but whose identities are weak. Barring previous bad experience, we prefer to deal with institutions we have heard of rather than those we haven't. The better known a school is the better it is liked and admired, and this very fact should serve as incentive enough to build and maintain a powerful identity program.

MISSION AND IDENTITY— WHAT'S THE DIFFERENCE?

Don't confuse mission with identity. Mission statements tend to be about being intellectually rig-

orous, responsive, caring, energetic and ethical. These statements reflect the wish rather than the reality.

The reality is that all schools already have an identity. Identity is a manifestation of what the school is all about, and in the end, identity is the responsibility of the people who run the institution and not only of its admissions, publications or public relations staff. It is more than just a way of labeling things or a sales slogan; it's a deep commitment to a particular way of doing education.

Because of their high visibility and impact, identity programs can signal turning points in a school's life.

IDENTITY PROGRAMS AS AGENTS OF CHANGE

Some school leaders fail to recognize the importance of identity management at all. While the publishing of this third edition of the *Marketing Handbook* indicates a growing enlightenment, the notion of marketing is relatively new and implementation is fragmented. Administrators are often blinded by the convention of what was done last year (or "down the street") and cannot see that things could be otherwise.

Nevertheless institutional identity programs are emerging as major agents of change. The impetus may be traced to the combined impact of declining demographics, rising costs (including demands for higher salaries and financial aid), depressed voluntary support, rising consumer expectations, and a shakier economy.

Because of their high visibility and impact, identity programs can signal turning points in a school's life. As you plan your school's efforts keep these three goals in mind:

1) *coherence:* the institution must present itself clearly and comprehensibly so that your multiple audiences understand how your programs relate to one another

2) *symbolism:* the school should represent its essence and attitudes, so that everyone who works for it can share the same spirit and then communicate it to all with whom they deal

3) *positioning:* the school must work to differentiate itself from its competitors in the educational marketplace

OBSTACLES TO INNOVATION

Keep in mind that little can be done about underlying identity issues until the school head gets involved and pushes for action. Olins' experience in the corporate world is that organizations engaged in relationships with smaller, better informed, more interested audiences can explain who they are more easily and economically than those with less engaged, mass audiences. Independent schools fit in the former group—but only insofar as their tradi-

All other things being equal, schools with good programs and powerful, well-coordinated identities will overshadow their rivals whose programs are just as good but whose identities are weak.

tional audiences are concerned. On one hand this may help explain the dearth of effort and resources that have gone into school communications programs. On the other hand, this puts schools in a better position to institute major innovations to their graphic identity.

There seems to be a bias on the part of many school leaders to play it safe and to do what the next school is doing. The inevitable result is that schools tend to look and sound alike, and even new logos and publications may reek of blandness. A further complication is that some design firms have developed a characteristic imprimatur while others may ape the current graphic mode. Design companies are strongly affected by peer pressure, and a lot of work produced intended to win appreciation from others in the trade subordinates the real interests of the client. Equally unacceptable and sadly abundant is the generic, unmemorable and therefore ineffective work done for half-committed institutions.

GETTING STARTED

Launching an identity program begins with listening to the different points of view of people inside and outside the institution. Although interviews and telephone or written surveys of individuals are the primary tools, many schools have found focus groups to be of value.

A *communication audit* examines how the school talks and listens and to whom. A *design audit* looks at how different parts of the institution

present themselves and how all that relates—if it does—to the presentation of the whole. A *behavioral audit* examines what it is like to deal with the school for those who come into contact with it.

LOGOS: THE HEARTBEAT OF GRAPHIC IDENTITY

Information gathered through the audits serves as the platform used by a professional creative team to develop a new school logo and subsequently other vehicles of communication. The ideal logo design reflects the dignity and tradition of the institution as well as its future. It must be sophisticated enough to convey the idea of quality education and yet not be stuffy. Technically, it must be simple enough to be reproducible in many forms and yet keep its design integrity and clarity. It must also be legible and memorable, because the logo serves as the heartbeat for the entire identity program. A designer for a new school logo would consider its multiple uses: that it will be worn on athletic uniforms, patches and t-shirts, printed on letterhead, notebook covers, blankets, mugs and jewelry, and painted on school vehicles and scoreboards.

MAINTAINING MOMENTUM

Identity programs either weave themselves into the fabric of the institution or they quickly unravel. Interestingly, the failure of a new design "look" is usually not because it is too radical, but rather that it was not properly introduced and managed over time. An identity program needs a power base across departments, and identity management brings with it the clear mandate that coherence and consensus replace traditional compartmentalization as the administrative ethos.

Implementation guidelines (a manual of graphic do's and don't's) accompanying the new logo artwork will help standardize and perpetuate the communications component of the identity program. But the ongoing vigilance of the head is needed to keep all the players in synchrony with the master plan.

The Next Marketing Handbook for Independent Schools

INSTITUTIONAL IDENTITY NITTY GRITTY

THE STAPLES. An institution's stationery should be printed on good (not opulent) quality stock, and all letterhead, cards, labels and envelopes should match. Schools who fail to coordinate the basics not only communicate managerial ineptitude but also may duplicate orders, spending more than they need to. Individuals and departments should be discouraged from having personalized letterhead to save money (names and titles typed in closing usually suffice).

During the summer, plan the coming year's stationery needs for all departments and order everything together, storage permitting. Outdated stationery should be cut down for notepaper or recycled. Contracts, permission forms, student reports, invoices and purchase orders should coordinate with the stationery.

Printers should be supplied with camera-ready art, Pantone Matching System®[2] ink colors and stock choices to avoid deviation from the new standards set and to assure consistency from run to run. Please note that ink printed on coated stock looks different from when printed on uncoated stock; you may need to work out a compensating mix with the printer depending on the actual job being printed.

COORDINATING SCHOOL COMMUNICATIONS

In the most sophisticated school settings, an individual supervises and coordinates these efforts. Titles vary from director of communications to director of external affairs to assistant head for advancement. This person, who usually reports to the head, will have a staff or assemble teams to work on specific projects. These teams may combine the talents of in-house people and professionals hired on an ongoing or project basis.

WRITING WITH YOUR READERS' INTERESTS IN MIND

More than likely a school can do some or most of the informational copywriting necessary for the major publications, such as student and faculty handbooks, course description books, newsletters and even student recruitment materials. Although the material may have multiple sources, one person

---

2. Pantone Matching System® is a registered trademark of Pantone, Inc. The Pantone Matching System is a standardized color communication system used by most printers. For more information, contact Pantone, Inc. (201) 935-5500.

The many homes of your school's graphic identity

Where are you likely to see a school's graphic signature? Everywhere. Here's a checklist:

- ✔ campus signage
- ✔ posters
- ✔ invitations and programs
- ✔ school vehicles
- ✔ team uniforms
- ✔ alumni/parent bulletin
- ✔ publications
- ✔ display ads
- ✔ gifts and school store items
- ✔ admission, alumni or development videos
- ✔ maintenance, housekeeping and student uniforms,

---

with editing experience should coordinate the total manuscript to guard against a toneless, writing-by-committee text. Any major changes in program, leadership or facilities should be anticipated in the copy to avoid producing a new piece that will be out of date soon after it appears. Review of final manuscripts by development and admission officers as well as an academic officer can help catch such potential problems.

Careful thought must be given to both public relations issues and market research findings in constructing a new text or in assembling the contents for an alumni-parent bulletin. Be careful not to overstate or exaggerate especially in recruitment materials. A school must be able to deliver what it promises in print (or video) or risk being called to task for false advertising.

Those working on the text must also remember that the finished product will fall flat with its audience if it is not written in a way that anticipates their questions, concerns, needs and motivations. More information on this topic is amply presented in David Treadwell's article, which begins on page 31.

BRINGING IN THE PROS

Because a school's identity is so dependent on graphic imagery, the institution will be well served by working with a professional design firm. The technical know-how and production contacts, as well as the creative touch which is the province of a highly trained, inspired inner eye, can combine carefully worded text and new photography into a smashing format that would be difficult or impossible for an untrained school staff member to achieve.

Creativity in Design

The dictionary definition of creativity doesn't say too much beyond the obvious that to create is to originate, to cause to come into existence, to make or to produce. My own experience suggests the following aspects of personality and production, which in various combinations make up creativity in design:

empathy—speaking to your audience, satisfying their needs

relevance—determining the purpose and function of the project in advance; honesty, directness

discipline/skill—of paramount importance! Gained through training and practice, experimentation, risk taking, success AND failure, understanding the conventions and production requirements of the medium, careful craftsmanship, steadfast adherence to high standards

boldness/surprise—using unexpected elements to gain your audience's attention

playfulness/humor—including visual and editorial puns to entertain the reader

imagination/inventiveness—combining or juxtaposing unrelated or unexpected elements to draw the reader in

devotion to beauty — carefully selecting elements for their composition, grace and visually pleasing qualities

collaboration—pooling talents and experience to make a team; virtually ALL creative people in communications mention that their work is strengthened through working partnerships

For myself, other important features of creativity include emotional investment in the work and a willingness to be critiqued. Most often both visual and text elements stand to be improved through the editorial process — "pruning and refining." — *C. C.*

The school should interview printers, agencies or freelancers offering design services to go over a prospective project. Preparing in advance for such meetings will enhance a school's chances of selecting the most appropriate professional for the job. The selection committee should have established the publication's:

- purpose
- audience(s)
- quantity
- distribution
- budget
- schedule
- graphic preferences and caveats

The school should be specific in outlining what it can provide (text, drawings, map) and what services the designer should provide (arranging for photography, design, production management, liaison with printer).

The school should seek written proposals addressing timetable, services to be performed, costs and other pertinent information, including contingencies. One individual within the school should serve as the liaison to the person or firm hired, and this person should be prepared to spend time during the summer, if necessary, to assist in bringing new publications to completion in time for the beginning of the new academic year.

Some guidelines must be established by the school regarding approvals—who will sign off on

What's it really going to cost?

If you want to keep your business manager off your case, remember to factor in *all* the expenses necessary to get a publication into the hands of your readers. Here's a checklist to follow.

WRITING

Do you use a part-time writer or do you offer honoraria to faculty members who contribute articles? If you hire someone to do a writing project, get an estimate in advance.

PHOTOGRAPHY

If you are hiring a photographer to shoot specifically for this job, remember to add in a sum for the per diem rate, film, developing and contact sheets, prints and out-of-pocket expenses. If you have a photography budget covering all of the school's major publications, you may want to set up an internal charge-back system, assigning a per print "fee" for photos actually used in each job. Check with your business manager. If you are doing your own photography, make sure to give yourself a film allowance and factor in the cost of processing when budgeting for a publication.

DESIGN

If you are using a freelance graphic designer, a design firm or your printer to do this part of the work, you can get an estimate in advance. Professional assistance on design is money well spent. Be clear on what the design services include (comps, typesetting, camera-ready mechanicals or final L-300 (high resolution printer) output to rc —resin coated—paper or film for desktop jobs, etc.).

TYPESETTING

You can get an estimate in advance for traditional or desktop publishing typesetting. You can reduce expense by keystroking your copy and submitting a disk and hard copy backup (save in ASCII file) for typesetting by your designer, a desktop publishing service bureau or certain printers. Or, your typed copy can be scanned to avoid rekeystroking. You can wreck your budget by changing copy after it has been submitted for typesetting (author's alterations). Get approval early!

CAMERA-READY MATERIALS

Traditionally prepared mechanicals are time-con-suming to assemble—make sure this cost is estimated in advance by your designer or the printer. Desktop publishing makes it possible to reduce mechanical preparation time significantly or to skip this step completely. For DTP jobs ask your printer if he/she wants final Linotronic output to rc paper or to film negatives; if you are providing film negatives there should be a reduction in the printer's prep charges (less camera work, less stripping). Get a price on Linotronic output from your DTP service bureau, and remember that rc paper is less expensive than film.

PRINTING

The quote should include prep work (camera, stripping, proofs and plates), stock, press time, bindery and shipping. Get separate bids on design/typesetting/mechanical work and mailing fulfillment. The printer will charge for author's alterations—this can cost big time—and for "overs" (up to 10% above the quantity you ordered) unless you agree in advance that you will not accept overruns.

MAILING FULFILLMENT

Depending on the job, this may include collating, inserting in envelopes, labeling, sorting, stamping, bundling, processing and dropping at the post office. Some schools maintain their mailing lists with a mailing house, so there would be a charge for generating labels or laser printing envelopes. Make sure to let the mailing house know how many "foreigns" there are when getting a price. (Are your permits up to date? Have you planned with the business office to obtain a postage advance?)

POSTAGE

Plan ahead and you will be able to mail more things nonprofit bulk rate.

OTHER EXPENSES

Permissions—fees to museums, libraries, newspapers for use of photographs. Photostats, illustration work, color photocopies, clip art. Express mail and faxes. Envelopes (magazines to overseas addresses must mail in envelopes). Insert cards (class notes, admissions, summer school) in magazines. Photo conversions.

Photo Freak-out

Last week a Cheney & Company editor was found foaming at the mouth after she unpacked a school's text and photos for a new issue of the school magazine. And why? The pictures were paper clipped together in batches for each article and captions had been written on the backs in ballpoint pen. Yes, there were scratches, and yes, the ink offset onto some of them. Of course, we've seen worse. We once worked with a school publications director who drew crop marks in ink onto the surface of each photo. Another well-meaning wretch **cut** the photos to the desired crop, meaning those pictures could never be used for another purpose.

When you are getting your visual materials together to present to the designer, here's the best way to do it:

• photocopy each shot

• type the caption on the photocopy and note which article the photo goes with

• if you have cropping or silhouetting instructions, mark them on the photocopy

• use pencil (write gently or photo will "dent") or indelible felt-tip pen (Sharpie) to mark information on backs of prints; you should catalog photographer, date, contact sheet and frame number and subject for further reference (some schools type this on labels and affix to back—that's ok, too)

When presenting photos to the printer with your mechanicals or Linotronic output (for desktop jobs):

• tape the photo to a sheet of white paper (one flap only at top of photo over white border—if no border make tape "loop" for back; tape over photo image will **show up** and if you ever try to remove tape you may rip image)

• write photo and/or job page number on the paper and the percent of reduction or enlargement

• cover photo with square of tracing paper taped to white paper and make crop marks or area to be silhouetted on this overlay—don't press hard

• there should be a photocopy of each picture reduced/enlarged, cropped and marked "fpo" (for position only) in place on the mechanicals as a guide to the stripper

STORING PHOTOS:

• contact sheets can be punched and kept in 3-ring binders; negatives, if you own them, should be stored in sleeves behind each accompanying contact sheet

• binders should contain an inventory of subject matter for all contact sheets (school service project); we suggest organizing chronologically

• store recent prints by subject in manila folders in a file cabinet

• store older prints in the school archives in acid-free boxes or folders (consult your librarian)

• store slides in sleeves in 3-ring binders; carefully write photographer, date, subject on slide mount using ballpoint or permanent felt pen (plastic) or pencil, ballpoint or felt-tip pen (cardboard)

• all school photography should be kept in one central location (except archival materials)— no hoarding by separate departments allowed

copy and photo selections, layout and proofs. Interference by well-meaning trustee committees and administrators can add significantly to the cost and production time, while possibly diminishing or diluting the project's overall impact.

ASSESSING YOUR SUCCESS

Once a publication is released for distribution, the school should work toward assessing its success from a number of standpoints: Did it come out on time? Is the quality of the printing and stock satisfactory? Did the job come in on budget? Is the publication stimulating the desired response or action on the part of the audience? If you had it to do over again, what would you change in the content, format or process?

CONCLUSION

Schools traditionally have shied away from "doing" public relations, publicity, advertising and more than the bare bones necessities in publications. They have turned a cold shoulder on comprehensive communications programs and have mistaken marketing for selling.

The fact is, however, that schools will derive huge benefits from managing their identities more effectively. I know of no school that can rest comfortably with the practice of haphazardly communicating if it wishes to keep enrollments secured for the years to come, to ensure generous voluntary support and to maintain the good will of its constituencies.

Schools wishing to strengthen their bonds with the community, to enhance their potential to serve a varied student body and to enlarge their resources—people, program, plant and purse—should think hard about how they present themselves on paper. Putting the "theory" to practice offers administrators, faculty, their friends and supporters an opportunity to exercise the ingenuity and resourcefulness that have long characterized independent education.

Carol Cheney works with independent schools nationwide on their communication programs and marketing strategies. Cheney & Company, her New Haven, CT based firm, produces alumni, development and admission publications. A former director of publications and public relations at Choate Rosemary Hall (CT), Carol also creates logos and conducts communications audits for schools, colleges, and other nonprofit institutions. She is a frequent speaker for The Council for Advancement Support of Education (CASE) and served as coauthor, editor and designer for The Next Marketing Handbook's *two predecessor editions.*

Doing it Desktop

Q. What is desktop publishing (DTP)?

A. Desktop publishing brings the processes of typesetting (composition) and preparation of page make-up together through the use of a personal computer. In this manner, DTP encompasses a number of prepress activities—typesetting, layout, graphic design, and color separation; it is *not*, however, a replacement for printing.

Q. How does DTP work?

A. First the text is typed in and corrected using a word processing program. Then, moving to a page format program, the copy is "poured" electronically into place on the pages using previously determined design guidelines. The copy can be rearranged or moved by pointing a stylus at the computer screen. Also, other graphic elements can be put in precise position electronically.

Q. What kinds of projects are best suited to DTP?

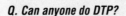

A. Forms, schedules, newsletters, invitations. For the operator with more experience, the system is effective for bigger jobs, such as viewbooks, magazines or annual reports.

Q. Can anyone do DTP?

A. Anyone can learn to operate the personal computer that makes it happen, but without design training and knowledge of the conventions of typesetting, the job will look amateurish.

Q. Is the quality of DTP good enough for all publications?

A. Laser printers print out copy with a resolution of 300 to 600 dots per inch. Even the naked eye can detect some raggedness. But the DTP disk can be played out in final through a Linotronic typesetter at 1270 dot resolution at a modest cost per page.

Q. Is there paste-up with DTP?

A. Documents printed through a Linotronic onto resin coated paper or film negative can be handed directly to the printer without paste-up. However, the document should be accompanied by a photocopy with photographs in place and color breaks indicated. If the printer is going to shoot the photographs, your L-300 output must be accompanied by the actual photographs and photocopies of them, noting cropping and sizing. Photographs and other graphics can be scanned into the document as low resolution files "for position only" reference purposes.

Q. Does DTP save time?

A. The text can be input and corrected once—there is no need to rekeystroke and proof the "typeset" version. Authors' alterations and changes to the layout can also be made on the fly—without waiting for outside sources to provide those services. However, documents produced using DTP run on generally the same schedule as those produced traditionally with a shift in time spent by an outside firm to time spent by a school staff member. In addition, offices making the switch to DTP methods should expect to spend more time on publications as staff gain familiarity with the programs and test their skills as typesetters and designers.

Q. Does DTP save money?

A. Yes—if the equipment is yours or if you can provide a DTP service with your clean copy formatted on a floppy disk. In both cases, you will save on typesetting. If you own your own equipment, you will also save on traditional paste-up. But, if you have to hire out the DTP service and cannot provide your copy on disk, the savings will be modest.

Q. How much does it cost to set up a DTP workstation?

A. The answer depends largely on your needs. The most basic setup, one which would allow you to get manuscript on disk, can be had for $1000 or less—if you are not averse to used equipment. From there costs range from $2,500 to $30,000 or more, depending on the use to which you plan to put the workstation, your technological capabilities, and your requirements in terms of memory, disk space and working conditions. At this stage you should consider talking with a consultant to determine the workstation that will suit you best—and cost you least.

Q. Who owns DTP files?

A. The DTP file is the product of the person or firm which creates it following trade custom on ownership of art mechanicals. Design firms using DTP who spell out their policies on file ownership in writing generally stipulate that clients will not receive copies of finished files without either prior consent or payment of a fee. If you know that you want a copy of your final DTP file, you should notify the design firm in advance. Disks submitted by a school to a DTP agency are the school's property. Such disks should be returned free of charge on request.

A Public Relations Primer

MARGARET W. GOLDSBOROUGH

It's safe to say that independent schools are no longer allergic to publicity. In fact, most schools now have either a public relations/information director or a member of the administration (often the development or publications officer) who is responsible for executing or coordinating publicity efforts.

Schools today recognize the value of publicity—that it is an important part of their overall marketing effort—even though it is difficult to quantify its benefits in terms of applications for enrollment or dollars in the annual fund. When a respected newspaper, magazine or TV station carries a story about your school's stellar science program, it has a credibility that your slickest catalog can't approach. It's "objective." When the news is bad, the good relations your school has cultivated with the press will help the school get fair, balanced reporting.

To be effective, the person charged with handling public relations needs support at the top and campus-wide ownership of the school's commitment to achieving greater visibility. Getting to know colleagues from every corner of campus life is key. They are the people who have the story ideas (even if they don't know it!); the PR person is the one who recognizes which stories will reinforce the school's message and then packages and sells the ideas.

PR TOOLS

There is no substitute for **personal contact**. PR people should introduce themselves and their schools to the reporters and editors responsible for covering education issues in the local and regional media. Consider dropping off a press kit with carefully selected materials describing the school, the head, and any particularly distinctive people or programs. If there's a chance to talk then or during a follow-up phone call, find out what kind of stories are of particular interest, whether they prefer phone calls or letters, and when the best time to call is to avoid interrupting near deadline.

A good PR person develops a strong **news sense**, finds the angle that will interest the media, and doesn't bother reporters with non-news. There's no quicker way to lose credibility, unless it's being so persistent that you are seen as a nuisance. It's important to get to the point quickly, whether it's on the phone, in a letter, or a press release. There will be time to expand on your themes later, if you have sold the idea. Be willing to share the story. If there's another source that could be valu-

Getting to know colleagues from every corner of campus life is key. There is no substitute for personal contact.

able on a particular story, tell the reporter. Your magnanimity will be rewarded when the reporter comes back to you for another lead.

A few rules to live by when dealing with the press: respond quickly if you can; always tell the truth; always speak "on the record."

The **media list** is a publicist's most valuable tool. There are a number of very good national directories which are available for purchase (quite expensive) or at the local library. Most major cities have a regional media directory, often published by the local chamber of commerce. Check with your opposite numbers at other schools and colleges—they may be willing to share their lists with you.

The main list should include: education and feature writers and editors, city editors, weekly editors and reporters, TV and radio news assignment editors, local wire service bureaus, and other regional and specialty publications. Over time, the PR office will develop sub-lists in addition: the call list of most valued contacts who would be phoned with breaking news; education supplement editors; calendar editors; TV and radio talk show producers; and public affairs directors. Be sure to keep the list up to date!

Press releases come in and out of vogue, according to PR consultants, but they are still a necessary, basic tool with a twofold purpose: to alert the press to an important event, trend or story, and to provide ready-made material for smaller media outlets which can use verbatim submissions. News releases should be double-spaced, written in journalistic style, i.e., with the most important information (the conclusion) at the beginning, followed by supporting information, in descending order of importance. Make sure that the name and number of the

contact person and a release date are prominently placed at the top of the release.

The Federal Communications Commission requires TV and radio stations to set aside a certain amount of time for free **public service announcements** (PSAs). By all means take advantage of that! Concerts, speeches, and other performances which are open to the public, book sales, and open houses are all likely subjects for PSAs. Time your PSAs to be read in a specific number of seconds—15, 20, 30—depending on the advice of the public service director at the station. Type the release entirely in uppercase letters, triple-spaced, with start and stop dates for airing and the timed length indicated at the top. Check with the TV station to see if it will, on occasion, provide its own personnel and studio for PSA production at no charge. Ask, too, if they will accept your professionally produced videotape with a voice-over, or your script-slide submission.

The **press advisory** is an invitation to the press to cover an event. It answers all those W questions clearly and succinctly: who, what, when, where, why. The **tip sheet** (or lead sheet) is a short list of story ideas, each presented in one or two sentences. These are especially valuable for education supplement editors and for reporters looking for "back-to-school" stories.

Approach **press conferences** with extreme caution! What could be more embarrassing than trotting out your top people for a press conference with no press? Unless you have a world-class star, it is very, very difficult to be sure that the press will come. Breaking news events—a multiple car pile-up, a raging fire, or pyrotechnics in the state legislature—can all draw away the press. For an individual school, the press conference's most likely value would come, unfortunately, in times of crisis when the school must respond to multiple, simultaneous inquiries.

If a press conference is in order, choose a room with ample space, decent acoustics, an attractive backdrop, and adequate electrical outlets and power for radio and TV equipment. Prepare press kits or fact sheets in advance, have a sign-in sheet for the press so you know where to follow-up, set the ground rules at the beginning of the conference. Will there be a statement? A question and answer period? Do reporters have access to the rest of your campus?

PRINT COVERAGE

Opportunities for coverage by **education writers** in major daily papers vary greatly—in some cities the person on the education beat has an understanding of the contributions of independent educa-

The Next Marketing Handbook for Independent Schools

tion and a willingness to write about the schools or at least include them in trend pieces. In others you may find anything ranging from ignorance to antipathy. It is important to keep information flowing to the education writers no matter what their predisposition, and at the same time look creatively at other opportunities at the paper.

Cultivate a relationship with **feature writers and editors**, keeping in mind that they, even more than the education writers, will be interested in the visuals your story offers. There's nothing quite like a colorful photo splashed across the front of a section of the Sunday paper to make your alumni, and potential parents and donors, sit up and take notice.

Keep the off-beat in mind, too. The food critic at one of Honolulu's major dailies wrote a big story on Hanahauoli School when they staged a special celebration for the 90th birthday of a retired school cook, sending out a strong message about the caring nature of their campus community. Hanahauoli also made good use of its connection to another paper's art critic, an alumnus, who did a fun feature on the school-wide art exhibit and fair, underscoring the school's mission-related emphasis on the arts.

Taking a fresh look at statistics led to inventive stories for two NAIS girls' schools. Girls' Preparatory School placed a nice piece in the *Chattanooga News-Free Press* based on their observation that they had become the largest independent girls-only secondary school in the United States. The Hockaday School in Texas lets people know that they are the largest nondenominational boarding and day school for girls, a fact which was noted in a major feature complete with photos and sidebars in the *Dallas Times Herald.*

Special sections offer wonderful opportunities for coverage of independent school stories. Education supplements are of obvious importance, but keep in mind that other sections such as sports and summer activities, for instance, could also use your ideas. Supplements usually have lead times months in advance and often accept freelance submissions. Ask about both well in advance.

Editorial writers and commentary columnists are open to hearing from readers. It's best to have the school head or a trustee write a letter (the PR person might ghost write) explaining why a particular issue is important to schools. It might affect the paper's editorial stance or the columnist's opinion, or call public attention to an issue that might otherwise be overlooked.

Op-ed articles (literally meaning opposite to the editorial page) provide schools with excellent opportunities for exposure. The op-ed editor is the contact person who can give you information about preferred length for articles and subjects of particular interest. A program in which the head, faculty members, trustees, parents and students take turns writing occasional op-ed pieces on timely topics can keep the school's name and position before the public. **Letters to the editor** are one of the most heavily read parts of any newspaper. Encouraging members of the campus community to write carefully crafted letters will increase your visibility.

The media list is a publicist's most valuable tool.

Simply keeping your school's name in front of the public can be very helpful. Use your local paper's **calendar columns** (be aware of long lead times in some instances) and **kudos** columns for special accomplishments of local residents. The importance of **local, suburban or weekly papers** should not be underestimated either. They welcome, and often print verbatim, news of residents of the area. Boarding schools often use hometown releases in distant cities from which they draw substantial numbers of students, noting total numbers as a part of their release on incoming students or graduates.

ELECTRONIC MEDIA

The key to getting **TV news coverage** of your school is to identify the exciting visual content that will give them good footage. (If you keep this in mind when you are planning your events, you'll probably plan better events, too!) Your contact is the news assignment editor, usually a different person for weekday and weekend news. Many noontime news shows have five-minute, live interview segments featuring a person from the community being interviewed by an anchor person. Check with the producer of the program and offer to supply a list of good questions if they are interested.

Radio news and feature shows are most likely to be attracted by "good sound." The news shows will often record phone interviews; the feature reporters are more likely to cover a campus story in person, conducting a number of interviews and recording background sound to lend color to the story.

Producers of **public affairs interview and talk shows** on both radio and TV are usually open to suggestions for good topics and articulate guests. A

Guidelines for Editorial Board Meetings

One important method for improving understanding of independent schools is holding meetings of school leaders with the editorial boards of local newspapers. Here are some guidelines for arranging, preparing for, and conducting an editorial board conference.

INTRODUCTION. The editorial board of a daily newspaper generally includes the editorial writers for the paper and is headed by the editorial page editor. This group almost always provides opportunities for members of the community to make appointments for the purpose of discussing issues of concern to that community. (At a smaller paper, members of the community might meet just with the editorial page editor.)

STRATEGY. To demonstrate the contributions of independent schools to your community, for instance, a group of two, three or at most four people might visit together. Candidates for the team might include heads of two very different schools— for instance, your state/regional association executive director, or a prominent school trustee from the community who is well-informed on independent education issues. (In some communities, it might be appropriate to widen your scope and include different kinds of private schools. If a regional CAPE affiliate is in place, that might be a logical starting point.)

ARRANGING THE CONFERENCE.

1. **Appoint a coordinator** to make the arrangements for the editorial board visit. Keep in mind that the coordinator will need some time to make arrangements with the team, but need not be the individual with the most influence at the local paper. Another person can be assigned to make the actual call or to sign the request letter to the paper, if that seems appropriate. While the call or letter requesting the meeting can come from a person with a personal friendship or special relationship with the paper, it is a serious mistake to expect that connection to do more than open the door. If invited to visit, it is important to respect the impartiality of the editors and not try to apply undue pressure, from advertisers for instance.

2. **Research.** Most leaders within the independent education community will already be aware of the attitudes of the local paper toward the schools, but stopping to reflect on that attitude and the kinds of coverage that appear can help shape both your request for an editorial board visit and the eventual discussion. Determine, too, whether the paper has strong biases against any particular institutions and avoid bringing such a representative to the conference.

3. **Recruit** your team of visitors, striving for representation of several sectors of the independent or wider private school world. Emphasize those organizations that have articulate leaders and the best information available about involvement with and contribution to the community. (Don't take your public relations people—editors would probably prefer talking with heads, trustees, or well-informed parents.)

4. **Contact the paper.** An influential member of your team of visitors should be assigned to contact the editor of the editorial page to request a meeting with the editorial board. The request can come in the form of a phone call or letter, depending on your contact person's style and personal relationships at the paper.

5. **Preparation** for the meeting is essential. Each member of the visiting group should be thoroughly familiar with the issue you wish to present and, most importantly, have concrete examples of the ways in which independent or private schools are benefitting the community. Be prepared to cite specific illustrations.

Some suggestions for information you might want to collect before the meeting include:

• total number of jobs generated by the presence of your schools, including a breakdown of professional, clerical and other support

• total spending by schools, including salaries, services, supplies

• total enrollment with an estimate of savings to the municipal or county school system by virtue of the removal of those students

• total financial aid given by the schools

• enrollment of students of color (depending on your area's demographics and school assignment process, private schools often offer greater diversity than local public schools)

• public/private partnerships in effect including joint academic programs with public schools, public/private school faculty cooperation

• availability of campus facilities for community events

• campus cultural and social events open to the community

The Conference. A meeting of this sort generally will not last more than an hour, and may be as short as 30 minutes. The editors will determine the format, but the visitors most likely will be asked to introduce their issue and then answer questions from the editors which will lead to further discussion. The tone of such a meeting is often quite informal and friendly. At the end of the meeting, if it seems appropriate, the visitors should ask for editorial support, but do not automatically assume that the paper will run a piece.

Follow-Up. A thank you letter from the person who initiated the contact with the paper should be written to the appropriate person on the editorial board.

pitch letter suggesting various ideas should be followed up with a phone call and an offer to supply more extensive background and suggested questions related to the topics that piqued their curiosity. That way you make the producer and interviewer's jobs easier, and your offer is harder to refuse!

On-air editorials and editorial rebuttals on both radio and television provide a platform for comment on public policy issues from any number of campus sources. Call the public service director to get the particulars on length of copy and taping arrangements. The public service director can also help you with arranging public service announcements about events and opportunities for the community on your campus. Opportunities on **cable TV** are many and varied, depending on your location. These are worth investigation if you have the staffing to handle it.

RESEARCH

The American public seems to have an insatiable appetite for polls and statistics and research findings. One of the almost surefire ways, then, to get your story told is to connect it to a new poll or report. A few recently completed and ongoing studies that might prove helpful are described briefly below.

The **National Education Longitudinal Study** (NELS) is a massive, long-term study by the U.S. government which aims to identify the circumstances under which American children flourish and succeed. Started in 1988, it is following the progress of 26,000 students from the eighth grade throughout their education. The researchers are re-interviewing and testing the same students every two years.

The most important feature of this study for independent schools is that the data for different kinds of schools—public, independent (NAIS members), Roman Catholic (parochial and diocesan), and other private schools—are all being reported separately. Thus, for the first time, independent schools can compare themselves quantitatively with other kinds of American schools. NAIS has provided member schools with information they can use based on the initial NELS findings related to course taking patterns and achievement results. Much more will be made available throughout the coming years. The results of the survey of these same students as 10th graders should be published in 1992. More extensive data from the detailed surveys of their parents and schools will be forthcoming as well.

NAIS polls

NAIS sponsors research from time to time on subjects of interest to member schools. The most re-

cent example is is a nationwide public opinion poll examining the attitudes of American parents about schools in general and independent schools in particular. Preliminary results of the first segment of the poll, which reported on families with incomes above $100,000, showed that these parents see individual attention and the presence of excellent, committed teachers as the most desirable characteristics of schools. Valued nearly as highly were an academic advantage for college admissions and an emphasis on integrity and building character. Compar-

---

The key to getting TV news coverage of your school is to identify the exciting visual content that will give them good footage.

---

ing public to private schools in nine areas, private schools were seen as doing better by large majorities in seven of nine areas. Preliminary results of this survey were first presented to member schools at the 1991 NAIS conference in New York, and subsequently made available in several formats.

Schools and staffing survey

Another federal study that will provide rich data is the Schools and Staffing Survey, nicknamed SASS. Seven questionnaires made up the initial survey, which examined school characteristics and factors that affect teacher supply and demand in public and private schools, including factors such as teacher satisfaction. 12,800 schools and administrators were surveyed, including 3,500 private schools and administrators. 13,000 of the 65,000 teachers surveyed were from private schools. Very little has been reported to date, but eventually schools will have access not only to aggregate data for public versus private schools, but for NAIS schools in particular, and various sub-groups of independent schools such as Episcopal schools, military schools, Friends' schools, etc.

Girls' school alumnae survey

In 1990, the 35-member Coalition of Girls' Schools commissioned a survey of 1,200 women who were alumnae of independent girls' schools. The researchers found that "single-sex secondary education gives women a significant edge over their peers in college and work." Their data debunked many popular misconceptions about girls' schools by citing the survey's favorable findings about goals, personal life, and career satisfaction, and their appraisals of the benefits of their single-sex schooling. Lots of publicity followed the issuance of the coalition's national press release with member schools helping to activate the press in their regions.

Other valuable sources

Teachers College Record, Vol. 92, Number 3, Spring 1991, Teachers College, Columbia University (special section on independent schools in the 1990s)

"National Study of Gender Grouping in Independent Secondary Schools," Valerie E. Lee, University of Michigan School of Education

Teachers at Work, Susan Moore Johnson, Basic Books, New York

Politics, Markets & America's Schools, John E. Chubb & Terry M. Moe, The Brookings Institution, Washington, D.C.

"Annual Gallup Poll of American Attitudes toward Education" published in *Phi Delta Kappan*

GENERAL ACADEMIC ISSUES

Successful school publicists find ways to peg their stories to national education issues and trends. There are various ways to keep up to date on the issues—reading the trade publications such as Education Week, *attending conferences, becoming involved with colleagues at other schools through regional and national associations. A few of the issues which seem likely to generate interest in coming years are outlined briefly below.*

Multicultural education

Multicultural education is one of the hottest academic topics for the 1990s. Education or feature writers might be interested in how your curriculum, library book selection process, or schedule of campus holiday celebrations reflects a growing awareness of the need for a broader multicultural perspective. If your school has undertaken the NAIS Multicultural Assessment Program, a thoughtful essay by the head might be accepted for your local op-ed page if it sheds light on how the community itself can address similar issues.

International education

Another theme that will be strong in coming years is international education. How is your school preparing students to live and work in a world featuring instant global communications and greater mobility? The addition of Asian studies programs at the precollegiate level will be of interest, as will any unusual language classes for children. Exchange programs with schools in other countries are a natural for press coverage. Green Fields Country Day in Tuscon, Arizona got extensive coverage for its exchange program with a school in Kiev, including an article in *USA Today*, multiple features and photo spreads in two major dailies, in area weeklies, and in the local parents' magazine.

Learning styles

Much current research is focusing on different learning styles. Some students learn visually, others aurally; some thrive as a part of a team, others work best alone. Certain investigators assert that today's students' brains actually function differently than those of a few generations ago, due in part to the faster paced, video-oriented world in which they are growing up. If teachers on your campus are experimenting with or employing new teaching methods, there might be a news story there. (Such an idea ties in nicely, too, with the overarching independent school themes about teacher empowerment and attention to individual students.)

Coeducation vs. single sex

Comparing the pros and cons of single sex and coeducational schooling is a subject of unending fascination to the media—most often when it's hooked to the release of new research findings or the announcement of a change in mission by a school or college. NAIS can provide member schools with national trend statistics about school mergers and moves to coeducation. Remember, too, that your school can generate publicity as a result of another school's news. If yours is a single-sex school and a nearby school is changing its mission to coeducation, consider an op-ed on why your school is not changing.

Moral and ethical education

Church/state separation contests in our courts have led, many would say, to an abandonment of moral and ethical teaching in our public schools, although some policy makers are now calling for a national effort to instill common teachings. Independent schools with and without religious affiliations have a 350-year history of success in this arena. Indeed, parents often choose our schools specifically because they provide an ethical community in which their children can grow and learn. How does your campus integrate ethical teaching into daily life? Does your school use materials or services from the multi-denominational Council for Religion in Independent Schools? The local press might well be interested.

Middle schools

The Carnegie Council on Adolescent Development calls the middle school "society's most powerful force to recapture millions of youth adrift" and asserts that "a volatile mismatch exists between the organization and curriculum of middle grade schools and the intellectual and emotional needs of young adolescents." If your school offers a model of good middle schooling, tell your regional or local education reporters about it. Referring to the Carnegie "Turning Points" study will give credibility to your pitch; the NAIS Middle Schools Handbook by Harry Finks of Lakeside Middle School in Seattle, Washington, can help you identify important themes to emphasize.

Other hot academic topics

Computers in the Classroom

Environmental Education

Learning Disabilities

Tracking

Sex & Drug Education

School Based Management

PUBLIC POLICY

Listed below are quick descriptions of a few of the public policy issues with which school heads and public relations directors should be familiar. These are issues on which you may or may not wish to seek coverage, but which journalists may bring up with you.

Choice in education

The debate over school choice has become a major item on the national education agenda. Whatever the fate of current reform proposals, the issue promises to shape the discussion for years to come. At this writing, the Congress is considering three proposals— the America 2000 plan with millions for new initiatives to foster parental choice programs involving private schools, the Senate Democratic bill with modest plans for public-only choice demonstration projects, and a House alternative. School groups across the country are watching with interest the choice programs involving nonpublic schools which are in place or being debated in the courts and legislatures in Milwaukee (WI), Chicago (IL), Epsom (NH), and the states of Florida and Delaware.

The heads of all NAIS schools have received a backgrounder on private schools and choice (July 1991 "Executive Summary") as well as a concise position paper on choice produced by the Council for American Private Education, the umbrella group representing most of the nation's nonpublic school groups (see box below). NAIS will be providing additional information to member schools as the debate continues.

Tax-exempt financing

A growing number of independent schools across the country are using long-term, tax-exempt bonds ranging from $1.5 to $30 million to finance major projects. Successful funding projects have been launched in Delaware, Massachusetts, Michigan, Minnesota, New Jersey, New Mexico, Oklahoma, and Pennsylvania. In some areas, such bond issues are arranged quite smoothly, but in others there have been debates in the media and the courts as to whether such funding comprises appropriate government aid to private schools. Schools generally argue that such financing is appropriate as recognition by the government of the contribution private

The Council for American Private Education Position Paper on Choice

Private schools by definition help fulfill the ideal of pluralism in American education. America's first schools were private schools established in the early 17th century. Today, twelve percent (5,391,000) of the nation's children are enrolled in private schools and thirteen percent (384,000) of the nation's elementary and secondary school educators are teaching in private schools. These schools are continuing to flourish and today are identified by strong statements of mission and purpose. They are religious and non-religious, large and small, urban and rural. They serve diverse populations, and are multi-ethnic and multicultural. Almost all vest the school's principal with the authority and the ability to implement change. Faculty, parents, and when appropriate students, are actively engaged in the decision making process. A sense of common community and common goals and an emphasis on values pervade these schools. The goals of private schools include academic excellence, meeting the needs of individual students and families, and a concern about the social, moral, spiritual, emotional, physical and intellectual development of each child.

As the nation becomes more focused on education reform, private schools provide significant models of success. They are ultimately accountable to the parents who continue to choose them. In 1925, the landmark Supreme Court decision, Pierce v. Society of Sisters, guaranteed the right of existence to non-public schools and therefore the right of parents to choose a school which reflects their values. The Council for American Private Education affirms this right and further urges national and state legislation which will provide all parents the opportunity to exercise fully their right to choose their child's school, religious, private, or public.

— *CAPE Board of Directors, October, 1990.*

schools make to society. Further, schools point out that such industrial development bonds are often used by other sorts of private corporations.

Tax issues

At any given time, there are a number of tax issues under discussion in Congress that have impact on the nonprofit sector in general and on independent schools in particular. Of special interest is the nonprofit sector's ongoing effort to permanently restore the favorable tax treatment of gifts of appreciated property. Other areas in which tax issues have affected or threatened to affect independent schools include auction tax deductions, "cafeteria" benefit plans, employer provided meals and housing, taxation of endowment income, financial aid, tuition remission, and the unrelated business income tax. The best sources of up-to-date information on these issues are the NAIS legislative affairs newsletters, business services newsletters, and development services newsletters sent several times each year to member schools.

Other public policy issues

Public Money in Private Schools

Length of School Year, Day

Teacher Recruitment

Child Care Licensing and Standards

National Volunteer Service

Teacher Certification

Americans with Disabilities Act

INDEPENDENT EDUCATION THEMES

Our public relations people often find themselves working to subtly educate the media about the independent school world. Listed below are some of subjects that pop up on their own, and some of the themes that PR people often try to stress with their media contacts.

Enrollment trends

One story that independent schools can count on every year is the enrollment trend piece. Over the course of the 1980s, independent school enrollment rose 2.2% despite a 0.3% drop in the number of school age children in the U.S. population. In 1990 and 1991, independent schools experienced continued enrollment growth, particularly in the lower grades.

Each summer, NAIS mails a detailed release with national enrollment and financial aid statistics, including trends for enrollment of minority and international students, to member schools and national media. Further information is available in the NAIS statistics summaries mailed several times each year to member school heads.

Financial aid

Tuition increases also seem to prompt annual coverage in the press; independent school publicists all need to work to be sure that the availability of financial aid is a part of the story too. In the last half of the 1980s, the amount of financial aid awarded by independent schools doubled, reaching $267 million in the '89-90 school year. A steadily growing percentage of students receive some form of aid, and more and more families are making use of creative financing options—tuition payment plans, low interest loans, and guaranteed tuition programs. It should also be noted that fund-raising for finan-

cial aid is one of the major thrusts of the development programs in most independent schools.

Accountability

Independent schools are not run by a central authority. Does that mean they are not accountable? School spokespeople who find themselves addressing this question may want to make some of the following points.

Independent schools have a long tradition of acceptance of fair and equitable government regulation in the vital areas of health and safety. In the areas of school management and academics, independent schools are rigorously self-regulating through several recognized associations of independent schools and six regional accrediting agencies. In addition, NAIS has established principles of good practice for areas of school operation with which member schools voluntarily comply. They include admission, instruction, governance, financial and business management, and fund-raising. Finally, unlike their public sector counterparts, independent schools are directly accountable to parents who choose schools based on performance and who withdraw their children and their financial support if a school fails to meet their expectations.

Other important independent school themes

Community Service

Parental Involvement

Value of Traditions

Greater Teacher Involvement

Individual Attention

Sports for Everyone

Campus as Ethical Community

Instilling Leadership

Margaret Goldsborough joined NAIS as director of public information in 1989 after four years as director of public relations and publications at the College of Notre Dame in Maryland. Earlier in her career she worked in a similar capacity for a Baltimore hospital and community college. A graduate of The Bryn Mawr School (MD) and Wells College, she has also studied at the Maryland College of Art.

NOTE: Selby Holmberg, former director of public information for NAIS and now director of external affairs, wrote the publicity chapter for the last edition of this handbook. Much of what is included in the PR tools, print and electronic media sections of this new chapter is derived from her earlier good work. —M.G.

Independent Schools Are Different

Independent schools are different in that their teachers interact with students not only as instructors in a classroom but as counselors, coaches, and leaders in all aspects of school life.

They are different in that curriculum is faculty determined, different in that teachers are accorded great freedom to teach in individual styles and to choose materials they deem appropriate for the particular students they teach.

They are different in that they are not comprehensive schools but are rather designed for distinct types of students in the community, be they the gifted, the middle of the road, the learning disabled, or those with special academic strengths.

They are different in that they are financed almost entirely by private means through tuitions, contributions, and fundraising activities. They do not seek public funding because they know that public funding brings bureaucratic regulation and with it the loss of the independence so vital to their academic success.

They are different in that they are actively self-regulating, actively promoting self-improvement through their member accrediting agencies.

They are different in that they are directly accountable to parents, and parents are actively involved in governance of the school. Independent schools which do not meet parents' standards do not last, because parents withdraw their children and with them financial support.

They are different in that they are free to seek the most effective ways to educate the particular children in their charge and in doing so provide for the needs of a diverse population. Different children learn in different ways. Different independent schools provide those ways.

— *John Esty*
NAIS President 1978-1991

Targeting Print Advertising

PRIVATE SCHOOL IS NO LONGER A LUXURY.

W hen it comes to your child's education, you want a school that adheres to a high-er standard. That's not a luxury, it's a necessity. ❀ These days, it's private schools that will challenge your child academically, provide individual attention, instill values and help develop full potential. Many of the best of these schools are located in Maine, New Hampshire and Vermont. The more than three dozen private schools of the North Country, from prestigious college preparatory schools to specialized day and boarding schools of all shapes and sizes, are located in the coastal cities and mountain towns of Northern New England, adding an exciting, outdoor component to your child's education. ❀ Even for families in financial need, our private schools are remarkably affordable. ❀ For a free directory of these schools, please call us toll-free at **1-800-654-EXCEL**. The Private Schools of Northern New England, P.O. Box 1871, Wolfeboro, NH 03894.

PRIVATE SCHOOL: CAN YOU AFFORD NOT TO?

SUE NICOL

WHO SAID TARGETING WAS EASY?

The U.S. Army recently tested a new weapons system intended to down attack helicopters. The computerized guns, mounted on a tank, were specifically designed to target whirling blades rather than heat sources as did the previous generation of such weapons. When the technicians pulled the triggers, the guns ignored all helicopter targets presented and obliterated instead the whirling blades of a nearby exhaust fan and the latrine to which it was attached.

The purpose of this chapter is to help you do a better job of targeting prospective applicants than this weapon did helicopters. In sharing the demographic analyses and advertising strategies that have enabled Oregon Episcopal School (OES) to mount several successful print campaigns, I hope to give other independent school marketers tools they might adapt to expand their applicant pools.

IDENTIFYING INFORMATION SOURCES

Several years ago I called a number of parents in our school community and asked them two questions: "To what magazines and newspapers do you subscribe?" and "What would be your first reaction if you saw an ad for Oregon Episcopal School in *Time, Sports Illustrated* or *Newsweek?*" Responses to the first question included those magazines plus *Forbes, Architectural Digest, The Wall Street Journal, Barron's,* various state and regional publications, *National Geographic, Smithsonian, U.S. News, Fortune* and the like. Reactions to seeing an OES ad included: "Proud," "Neat," "Spendy," "Validates my investment in an OES education," "Wow," "My school is in the Big Leagues," "The school is important beyond this community," and "The school must be doing something right." I was intrigued with the psychology of school name-association and the feelings of pride this apparently generated.

The Media Network offers direct placement of ads at greatly reduced rates in national publications going to subscribers within specific geographic/demographic boundaries. Armed with a desire to validate the OES experience to those within and without the school community, we placed an OES ad in the Media Network's subscription package. The cost for a full page ad in each of 7 major national magazines was half a boarding tuition, and well worth it.

Complementing the Media Network, we ran similar ads in major newspapers in Washington, Oregon, Idaho and Alaska. Ads published in local newspapers featured photographs and captions of the students who had enrolled from the communities served by the papers. Headlines included:

• "We're all going to college."

• "You won't believe what we're reading in the ninth grade at Oregon Episcopal School."

• "This is a partial reading list for ninth graders? Of course it is— at Oregon Episcopal School."

Another of our successful ads featured was headed: "Seize your opportunities at Oregon Episcopal School." The ad documented the successful outcome of an OES education for a young woman now enrolled at Vassar. Among the key quotes was this comment from Vassar's Associate Director of Admission: "Vassar looks for students who make a difference; Rebecca learned how to at OES and is continuing to do so here."

DOCUMENTING YOUR SCHOOL'S WORTH

In each of these ads we documented the worth of an OES education through the six marketing planks of the school: college placements, academic pace, small classes with individual attention, exceptional faculty, nurturing environment and moral values. The development of the stratagems came through research in which we asked the OES parent body why they had chosen our school. These results were then compared with the market research data coming from the NAIS PIE "Briefings" (see the Databank at the end of this book) and local demographics. We also looked carefully at the scope and sequence of the curriculum at various grade levels in local public and private schools and compared it to our own. The text of the ads included research-supported statements reflecting what the school does best and what our tuition-paying clientele expects of us:

"At OES we think it is as important for our 9th graders to read Kalidasa's *Shakuntala* and *The Chinese Wisdom Literature* as Homer's *Iliad, A Separate Peace* and *The Trials of Socrates.*"

"We teach Global Citizenship — walking in someone else's shoes."

"What you do in high school will determine the quality of your life for years thereafter!"

"Aside from your love and guidance, the only real gift you can give your child is a great education. It is the quality of this education that will determine the choices available in his or her adult life."

"We guide with a love which is kind and tough and tells the truth with the heart."

Other advertising initiatives using the same message include:

• A direct mail list from the Department of Motor Vehicles targeting high-end automobile owners who also own a Jeep Cherokee as the second car. Why this combination? There is a direct correlation between individuals who own this particular Jeep model as their second or third car and the higher income brackets.

• The profile of an OES student (accomplished French horn player and nationally ranked fencer) in the Oregon Symphony program handed out with each performance during the season.

- Sponsorship of a Science Lecture Series in the city of Portland. The ad reprints read, "Look who's coming to our campus this year." We then noted that our student body would enjoy conversations with the likes of Dr. Richard Leaky (paleoanthropologist), Dr. Robert Ornstein (neuro-psychologist), and Dr. Ian Stewart (author of the Chaos Theory).

*Validation of worth is **the** reason we document our 9th grade reading list in our ads, the reason we publish the college acceptance list, the reason we talk about our small class size and the quality of the experience beyond the academic range.*

Validation of worth is **the** reason we document our 9th grade reading list in our ads, the reason we publish the college acceptance list, the reason we talk about our small class size and the quality of the experience beyond the academic range — from moral values and intellectual risk-taking to our indoor tennis courts and all-weather surface running track. We have carefully considered that which we do well and in an unabashed manner we have discussed this with those who seek something more for their children.

As important, we have attempted to communicate this information to those who don't know we exist or who have not considered such an option. The goal, of course, is to expand the marketing niche and widen the loop. Though we complement with a variety of advertising forms, we use magazine and newspaper print ads as the most effective channel to carry our message to those outside of our parent/alumni referral and personal networks.

Independent schools should be, *must* be, educational flagships on the cutting edge of academic excellence. But we must also make a difference for *each* student enrolled. Whether your school best serves students who are marching off to competitive colleges or those with below average skills needing tutorial support, it is keenly important to identify what you do well.

LOOKING BEYOND GLOOMY STATISTICS

Although statistics depicting a declining traditional applicant pool discourage many admission officers, I prefer to focus on the still-expanding "new market/first generation" populations. If you really want to understand population trends for the 90's and beyond, look to folks like Gerber Baby Products who spend millions researching just that topic:

"During the last four years, births have increased each year and are forecast to be up almost 4% in 1990. After declining in the early 1970's, the number of births have trended irregularly upward since 1975. Early Bureau of Census projections called for declines in both 1989 and 1990; Gerber's assumption is that births in the US will remain in the four million plus range for at least the next several years. If births continue to rise, then the market could be up by a larger percentage. The bottom line is that better times are ahead, and they could be 'a lot' better."

The bulk of the US population is now comprised of individuals coming into their prime earning years. Although this group's affluence will wax and wane with booms and recessions, we should see more families who can afford educational choice thanks to increasing discretionary income.

MONITOR YOUR ECONOMIC MICROCLIMATE

School marketers should read business publications to learn of new ventures coming into their regions, as well as employment trends and new capital investments. Are you promoting your school in a healthy area? Don't forget that most independent schools must first have a stable population of full fee-paying families if the ideal scenario of an economically and ethnically diverse student body is to occur. While some may be concerned about the

"Buying of America" by foreign investors, independent schools should look to this as a boon.

The housing starts in a region can correlate with the enrollment trends of independent schools. Keep in mind that the population pool is increasing at a faster rate than the availability of independent schools. This pool is spending more money on housing, on goods and services, on education, on health care, and on investments and savings. Parents may be more willing in the 90's to buy the concept of independent education if the cost is validated by the school's ethos.

POSITION YOURSELF AGAINST PUBLIC SCHOOLS WITH DISCRETION AND INTEGRITY

While independent school marketers should never denigrate local public schools, it is equally important to clarify for the public both the standards associated with NAIS membership and the positive outcomes for the kids who enroll in our schools. I recently shared the following persuasive statistics with our Long Range Planning Committee: the largest public high school in the state of Oregon has a senior class of 1000 students with 3 National Merit Finalists. The OES Class of 1991 has 46 students with 5 National Merit Finalists and twenty-one percent of the class named in the National Merit Scholarship competition. After pondering what these facts might mean to individuals who know nothing about OES or independent education we wondered if there was any way we could use this information in telling the public who we are and what we do.

The challenges facing local public school boards include overcrowded classrooms, diminished extracurricular programs, high drop-out rates, poor college acceptance records, bureaucratic webs, and a perceived lack of values in the instruction process. These factors are among those that motivate parents to seek out educational choice. Roger Porter, Assistant to President Bush on Education, points out that, "After four years, only 17% of those graduating from high schools in the United States meet the requirements outlined in *A Nation at Risk*."

Such prospects are discouraging for parents expecting reasonable choices for their child after high school. In communities with struggling public schools, independent schools are being viewed as "no longer a luxury." "Private school: can you afford not to?" was the effective theme of the "EXCEL" advertising campaign recently undertaken by

the Independent Schools Association of Northern New England. Over 30 schools joined forces to expand their applicant pools, hiring Baltimore marketing firm Barton-Gillet to create the ad reproduced on page 54.

PROJECTING YOUR IDENTITY

As Bruce Buxton illustrates in Chapter 2, all truly effective marketing is rooted in a school's ethos. At OES all our promotional themes reflect our institutional identity as articulated in our statement of purpose — who we are and what we do! Mindful of our twin goals of recruitment and retention, OES's systematic advertising projects our identity message to both enrolled and prospective families.

NAIS data supports our conclusion that educational quality is the single most important factor for parents weighing educational options. Other factors include quality of the faculty, the academic standards of the school and the concrete outcomes. Don't underestimate the need to weave these four themes into the promotion of your school. Before you can tell others about yourself, you need first to know who you are, whom you serve and what you

With the exception of his parents, few individuals will have such a profound effect on a child as his teachers. That's why at Providence Country Day, we have made every effort to assemble a superlative faculty. Many of our teachers are, in fact, very gifted scholars. Just as important, they're also dedicated educators who will take the time to make sure the boys in this school learn as much as they're capable of. And sometimes a whole lot more. For information on admission requirements for boys, grades 5-12, call our Director of Admissions Mr. Kurty at (401) 438-5170.

THE PROVIDENCE COUNTRY DAY SCHOOL · 1923 ·

THERE'S NO TELLING HOW LONG THE INFLUENCE OF A GREAT TEACHER CAN LAST.

THE · REPUBLIC

PLATO

NAIS
MEMBER
Member, National Association of Independent Schools

Our target audience:
a demographic and psychographic portrait

The first step in targeting your advertising is to understand demographic trends at both the national and regional level as well as in the cities and towns from which you draw significant numbers of students. You should also have some idea of how your target populations spend their discretionary income. The following portrait emerges from my market research involving families from the Pacific Northwest, California, New York, Maryland, New England, the Midwest and Texas. Background data is drawn from *Fortune* and *Money* magazines, Associated Press and national polls reported in various newspapers, and PaineWebber research publications.

This is an upwardly mobile group of individuals in their forties who are baby boomers and who account for half of the country's adults. They will be sending children to expensive colleges, buying late model cars (finding the Lexus and Infiniti particularly appealing), investing in the stock market and their 401(k) plans while at the same time shopping at discount food and fabric stores and spurning expensive designer labels. If necessary, they will tend to stay in their present homes and remodel rather than purchasing more expensive dwellings. They have higher installment credit debts than 10 years ago but make every attempt to reduce them. Few of these families are succeeding in saving the significant portion of their income required to fund their kids' education and their own retirement. They spend less on liquor and wine, eat fewer meals in expensive restaurants, and make more charitable contributions.

This group of individuals enjoys professional, business or corporate status, is able in growing numbers to articulate a faith in God (though they may not be churchgoers) and a need for adherence to moral guidelines and values in society. They spend money on children (their own and others), and subscribe to the concepts of global citizenship and internationalism. While they may at times be overindulgent with their own youngsters, they expect schools to guide with a love which is tough yet supportive. They think pollution is a grave threat to both health and the environment and see environmental awareness as crucial to the long-term success of business and industry.

They embrace fitness and hard work, are members of health clubs, enjoy college and professional sports and, though seldom able to do so, like to attend professional basketball games. They are a print-addicted cadre who harvest their daily required dose of news from their local newspapers (often their closest big city edition), and perhaps one other publication including *The Wall Street Journal* or *Barron's*. They enjoy professional publications, sports and news magazines and best sellers. They view new movie releases from the local video store more often than they go to the movies, but their children do both. Half the moms work. In contrast to the 1980's, these folks seek to avoid conflict through mediation. They enjoy travel and often bring the kids along.

This group comprises the majority of individuals likely to enroll children in independent schools in the 90's. By and large, however, it is also the group which tends to send their kids to suburban public high schools. As *Fortune* magazine noted in a recent issue, looming college expenses are their economic *bête noire*:

> "The crunch is college. Giving their children the best possible college education is a cherished goal for most American executives. It's more important than the house, more important than anything. The majority of this group choose private colleges, where the average annual cost is now $16,000 for a non-Ivy League school. Putting two children through Ivy League schools starting in 1998 would require saving $12,214 a year for the next 14 years. Often parents have to drastically scale back their lifestyles, and they borrow from retirement savings or by taking out home equity loans."

As this group becomes more disenchanted with the public school sector, they will continue to seek out educational options. Economic pressure, though, may find them approaching independent school enrollment with trepidation. Documentation of our schools' worth and concrete outcomes have significantly more interest to this group than those at higher or lower income levels.

We must target this upwardly mobile group of parents with their preferred information gathering medium. They are ideally suited to print advertising, since they tend to settle in urban areas because of employment advantage. And even though a number of your parent body may be from small town USA, they are likely to live within 75 miles of a major metropolitan area and subscribe to that city's daily newspaper as well as reading big name magazines. In the state of Oregon, much of our new population comes from city dwellers escaping the social and environmental problems in other states, a trend that is expected to accelerate. The urban tilt happening across the country makes print media advertising just that much easier and more productive.

do best in the increasingly competitive educational market of the 90's.

The author acknowledges ideas and information drawn from the following publications:

PaineWebber, Portfolio Managers' Spotlight, 1990/91 issues

Oregon Business, The 10th Anniversary Issue, February 1991

Fortune, "America's Economy," March 11, 1991

NAIS Briefing, No.2, December 1990

The New York Times, The Wall Street Journal, The Oregonian

Money Magazine, April 1991

Sue Nicol has been the director of admission and a member of the trustee marketing committee at Oregon Episcopal School (OR) since 1982. Her fresh and effective print advertising and insightful targeting have attracted national attention. She is a past chair and steering committee member of the Western Boarding Schools Association, where she helped to develop marketing strategies and inquiry tracking systems based on the region's complex demographics. Sue serves on the faculty of the NAIS Admission Workshops and the SSATB Evaluation Committee.

Audiovisual Marketing for Independent Schools

TOM GRIFFITH

An admission director, wan with care, haunted by numbers, seeks comfort on a hillside overlooking the campus. Its beauty stirs him afresh; it awakens a world of glad memories; and he thinks, not for the first time, "O! If only they could **see** what I see, **hear** what I hear, **feel** what I feel! Then, they would apply in droves!"

Well, now they can. Of course they always had the option of visiting your school; but few did, and their impressions were subject to vagaries of weather, time and level of activity. Today, courtesy the Video Revolution, they may visit without leaving home. And their impressions can be artfully shaped in advance, in a medium that surpasses all others in capturing attention, touching the heart and sparking decisions.

This chapter will review the steps by which schools enter into this revolution. After briefly noting the arguments for video marketing, it will proffer advice in four areas: deciding what identity to project, choosing between slide/tape and video, selecting a producer and, most critically, distributing the final product. It's fine to make the show, but the show must go out. We will conclude with some state-of-the-art techniques of gaining maximum exposure for a school video.

WHY VIDEO MARKETING?

That schools must compete is not to be lamented; the discipline of the free market acts always as a spur to greater effort and superior products. It especially undergirds the dazzling creativity of American advertising, where much of our national aesthetic impulse seems to go. Video marketing of schools is a recent and noble entrant in this tradition, and while it can never supplant traditional recruitment means, it can provide a valuable new arrow in your quiver.

"But who will see it?" you ask. In 1986 a third of American households had a VCR; the figure is by now likely close to half. Increasingly, Americans not only use it for entertainment but to determine major purchases. Young people in particular are video-oriented, as accustomed to popping in a black cassette as to tying their shoes. Regrettably, they will be far readier to seek information on a school via visual rather than print media; but that's all right, as long as one leads to another.

"But isn't it too expensive?" you ask. Although the initial outlay for a video is indeed high, its cost per copy can be less than that of a glossy color viewbook. In 1991, producers estimate a range between $20,000 and $50,000. Yet as many admissions directors note, this expense can be recouped with even one or two extra admissions owing to the video. It's an investment, but usually a prudent one. The consensus grows yearly that when properly produced and distributed, videos work as marketing tools.

But isn't this a cave-in to the MTV culture? Not really. When school videos ape MTV's vacuity (and some do), they fail. When they reflect a serious investment of thought, love and craft, combined in a way that truly captures a school, they succeed. Video can attain to the same Parnassian heights as any other art form, and should not be prejudicially dismissed by the tradition-minded. Now on to the nitty-gritty.

DECIDING THE IDENTITY TO PROJECT

We begin with two axioms, drawn from Socrates and from basic rhetoric: know yourself, and know your audience. It may seem a simple enough business to record your school on tape, but it's not. You have to choose what to show and what to say, and you can't even begin that properly until you decide who's going to see it.

To keep the horse before the cart, therefore, consider the question of "audience." We assume that your main purpose is to recruit students; they are therefore the target. But are they the only ones? Do you also intend to show it to alumni, parents, professional associations, community groups, or your local cable outlet? Do you hope to use it for development purposes?

Veteran producer Mark Edwards offers this advice:

"It's important to keep the marketplace in mind when one is considering making a video. Research is critical, because it will help the producer understand the role the video needs to play in the communications process. For example, does the school really compete with other independent schools, or does it compete

Courtesy of Warner & Forman

Courtesy the Video Revolution, they may visit without leaving home. And their impressions can be artfully shaped in advance, in a medium that surpasses all others in capturing attention, touching the heart and sparking decisions.

with local public schools? The answer to this question will have a dramatic impact on the kind of video that's created."

How can the concerns of the intended audiences be known? Professional admission officers develop a good sense of what motivates young people to apply to their schools. Even with experience and intuition as their guides, however, many admission veterans now reinforce their perceptions and interpretations with market research. Marketing consultants can describe how the school is perceived by prospective applicants and their families. Too academic, or not enough? Liberal or conservative in lifestyle issues of dress and discipline? Caring or competitive? Too expensive, or within reach of middle-income people? Good researchers go beyond just quantifying perceptions — they make sense of them and work with a school to develop strategies based on the findings.

At this point, cart meets horse and the concern with audience blurs into the question of a school's identity. This isn't an obvious issue. Market reserch can indicate how the school appears to others, but the reality is best defined through hard thinking and discussing by those who know it best. Mark Edwards sees this post-research thinking as a critical step:

> "When market research confirms that prospective students think of your school as 'preppy and elitist,' you need to think hard before figuring out the best approach to countering this. It may *not* mean that your tape should have students saying, 'We're not preppy and elitist; we're very accessible,' as many tapes do. Perhaps the entire way that the tape is put together should counter the elitist perception."

Know yourself, and know your audience.

There are many aspects of a school's identity — its history, location, traditions, the character of its head, students, faculty, staff, and alumni. Those identity factors of a numerical or extremely factual nature are best left to catalogues and other print media. It is the *affective* aspects of identity that audio-visual programs must address.

One producer recommends settling on just four or five themes. If they are genuine, these themes needn't be contrived, but rather uncovered. For example, a school may have exceptionally close relations between faculty and students that can be shown through classroom scenes or testimonials. Or it may stress sensitivity to the environment and have a strong outdoor skills program, which gives great potential for dramatic footage. The themes must be genuine and clear, an honest reflection of the distinctive qualities of the school. Says one producer: "It is my experience that many, many independent schools are excellent. Your script must show what is different, what is 'special' about your school."

SLIDE/TAPE OR VIDEO?

Having established the themes of its identity, the school now confronts an aesthetic dilemma that it probably didn't know existed. The issue is between "live-action" productions (video or the rarely-used 16mm film) and slide/tape; between images that move and those that don't.

The older form is slide/tape, which has come a long way from the living room travelogues that figure painfully in everyone's memory. Some may be surprised that it has survived, and wonder why anyone would prefer it over video. But when samples are viewed, its distinctive advantages grow apparent. Those might be summed up in a single word: *more*. A fifteen-minute video might have forty or fifty different scenes. A comparable slide/tape show can have five hundred. Every still photograph reveals a different face, a different building, a different season. If you liken a school to a revolving crystal, slide/tape can show far more of its facets. The images are flashed rapidly, for seconds or less, but the pace can be varied and a sense of abrupt change muted by the technique of slow dissolve.

More also applies to a simple point of logistics — the screen for a slide/tape show is much larger than any television screen. An image twelve feet tall inevitably has more impact than one measured in inches; it envelops a viewer, overpowering distractions and intruding more forcefully into the imagination. On the other hand, a slide/tape show can easily be transferred onto videotape; that eliminates the logistics problem of extra projection equipment, but at the expense of having the images diminished in size and sharpness. A final advantage of *more* is hard to define, but most students of the form agree that slide/tape gains an advantage by its very inability to project movement. It offers instead a series of still images, on each of which the viewer is allowed to dwell for a moment. Whereas moving film virtually takes over the imagination, a slide engages and works with it. It suggests rather than insists, often inducing a mood of reflectiveness that suits an entity like a school, whose essence is more perceptible to the heart than the head.

For all that, video remains the preferred medium, and little wonder. The force of its illusion is unsurpassed, for it puts the viewer *there*. If it co-opts the imagination, most of us yield it up willingly, for it transports us through time and space as nothing else can. Its eye becomes ours, probing and peeping, beholding just the right setting at just the right time. If its effort to portray a school is success-

The Next Marketing Handbook for Independent Schools

ful, it leaves us thinking we've actually paid a visit. Video is especially attuned to youth, whose systems and imaginations run at higher speed than those of their elders. Slides may elicit a reflective mood, but video acts as a stimulant; its turbulent movement quickens mental activity and provokes an excitement that even registers physically. Just observe the effect of good sports footage on the heartbeat.

This trait is both video's peril and promise. But insofar as schools *are* exciting places, there's nothing wrong with reflecting that on tape. Those aspects of school life that involve students physically — sports, performing arts, mealtimes, work programs, other recreation — can be shown compellingly through video.

CHOOSING AND WORKING WITH A PRODUCER

Now more quandaries: why go "professional" instead of doing a video in-house? Which style of producer: high-powered commercial or low-key "artistic?" Is a background in education useful? What about the personality factor? Some institutions, especially rich ones, have excellent communications programs with facilities to produce their own promotional materials. Some of the results are very good. But by and large, a home-made depiction of the school looks home-made; and despite the charm that may impart to it, it won't compare well with other programs that are professionally produced. Remember, this show is often the first view of a school that many people ever get, and it may be the only view. An amateurish production can be worse than nothing. While it will probably require more money, time and trouble, the investment in professional production will pay off in the end.

To determine producer styles, it's vital to view their work. Some are geared more to business and industrial clients who employ them to introduce a new product or to profile a company for stockholders. Other producers regard themselves primarily as artists and strive for effects more popular in art cinema or public television. This has its own hazards; the results can tend toward the soporific, a danger with young viewers. But it's worth seeing a wide range of styles before choosing. Schools are in a good bargaining position, for the video business is booming and crowded with competitors, all of whom aim to please.

Be conscious not only of style, but of the producer's personality. Rapport is important, since an audio-visual project inevitably intrudes on a school's routine. It's like a temporary marriage, and

schools are only sensible to consider the personalities involved as well as résumés. If a certain producer comes off as too pushy, or too passive, if there doesn't seem to be much communication occurring or any excitement generated, keep looking.

BRAINSTORMING

When a contract is signed, the initial brainstorming can begin. Producers are unanimous in stressing the need for planning things out in detail.

If a certain producer comes off as too pushy, or too passive, if there doesn't seem to be much communication occurring or any excitement generated, keep looking.

There are roughly two phases to this process: conceptualization, and the writing of a script. The first phase enables school personnel and producers to get acquainted and thrash out general themes for the production. Since everyone on earth secretly wants to make movies, there should be no lack of ideas about what would be of cinematic interest. For example, what settings on campus are most alluring? What students or teachers would give a good interview? Most important, what distinctive qualities of the school should be highlighted? The process ought not to be rushed, and those involved should be giving some hard thought to the questions before any meetings take place.

SCRIPT

Next, a rough plan of actual scenes can be developed. It should be noted that a "script" here does not necessarily mean dialogue or spoken narration; in fact, the less of that, the better. An effective script will instead list locations, events, interviews, settings. Don't be surprised at resistance to determining in advance the verbal content of a program. The best producers strive to allow audio-visual to do what it does best — win the viewer with unrehearsed moments that engage eye, ear, and heart directly. These moments are the A-V equivalents of what visual artists call "found art."

For example, an unplanned humorous exchange in a dorm room can tell more about the atmosphere of a school than the most eloquent direct statement by the headmaster. And the effect of that

exchange may not even be evident at the time it's recorded. That's why producers shoot massive amounts of tape, guided loosely by a script but equally by their artistic instincts. Only later, when hours of tape or hundreds of slides are sifted through in the editing room, do these jewels of spontaneity appear. So give latitude to producers — some scenes that look promising on paper fall flat, while others that were just stumbled upon work beautifully.

Think "distinctive." One school in Connecticut overlooks a bend in a river. That accident of geography was used for a powerful metaphor on the way student's lives flow toward the school, mingle with it, then flow away again. Every school has some such feature, so think what it may be in your case.

INTERVIEWS

A byword among producers is to let schools "speak for themselves." Not narrowly, through prepared statements of an official, but broadly, through unrehearsed remarks of the widest possible sampling of the entire community. Since the primary audience will be potential students, it is students whose voices should be most prominent. As we know too well, peers influence peers more than anyone else. Second in importance are the faculty. Surveys of independent school applicants show that the "quality of teachers" is *the* major determinant of a choice of school. And little wonder — they are among the most gifted and dedicated members of the profession, many of whom have traded the higher wages of public schools for the close relations and sense of common purpose to be found in independent institutions. They are the key to a school's success, and ought to be showcased proudly.

FOUND SOUND

While we think of film as principally a visual medium, its practitioners know that much of its power to move us derives from the soundtrack. What strikes the eye may get our primary attention, but much of our response is governed by words, music and ambient sounds. Just as there are char-

acteristic sights to a school, there are characteristic sounds — the tolling of the chapel bell, the whir of a pottery wheel, shouts at a soccer match, the pelting of rain against a dormitory window. These contribute a realistic texture to pictures of the same things. A skillful producer has a keen ear for found sound.

PHOTOGRAPHY

Now for the "visual" in audio-visual. Much depends, of course, on the medium — the rules for slide/tape are quite different from those for video or film. The common link is the need for quality. Some schools have an archive of slides or film that they want incorporated into a program. That may work fine, but they should not hope to save costs by using amateur pictures in lieu of professional ones taken for the purpose. Quality photography is the name of the game, the bare minimum on which a good audio-visual program is based. Professionals expect to discard a large percentage of what they shoot in order to come up with the most attractive portrait possible, and schools should anticipate that.

MUSIC

As noted before, music helps set the tone of a program and can be used to manipulate a viewer's responses. Lively, fast-paced instrumentals can grab his or her attention, but can also numb it if continued too long. Slower, meditative music can help vary the rhythm and provide good background for scenes showing arts classes, for example. Different kinds of schools are reflected in different kinds of music: drum and bugle for a military academy, classical for the highly academic, modern jazz for the nontradi–tional. Producers also draw on a vast array of recorded work called "library" music, where the right sound is bound to be found.

EDITING

This step takes place entirely apart from the school, yet is the most crucial of all. The process is highly technical and highly tedious. It entails the running and coordinating of hours of tape, each segment measured in seconds. The all-important transitions between scenes are wrought, to give a smooth flow to the production. Fifteen to twenty hours of recording are distilled down to twelve to fifteen minutes of the final program. Here more than anywhere is the skill of your producer tested, for a program lives or dies by what happens in the cutting-room. Usually a "rough cut" is assembled and shown to the school personnel responsible for

The Next Marketing Handbook for Independent Schools

the project, for comment and revision. The producers then return to their laboratories, to emerge days later with the final product.

DISTRIBUTION

After celebratory showings to students, alumni and others, it's time to put the tape to work. As video's cost per copy drops to rival that of color viewbooks and catalogs, some boarding schools have begun to mail a video to all inquirers. Other logical recipients of your tape include "feeder" schools, public or private, that regularly receive the school's publicity.

Many counseling offices have acquired video libraries from which students may choose. There are numerous other avenues — personal contacts through alumni or current students (never underestimate the power of "word of mouth"); conventions or other public gatherings, where everyone welcomes a chance to relax into a film; local cable outlets, whose schedule may afford a free showing. Perhaps the most valuable of these contexts is the current parent reception. Savvy admission officers use the video as both lure and ice-breaker at these neighborhood gatherings hosted by those most effective of school salespersons, satisfied current parents.

A notable innovation in video distribution is the *Boarding Schools Directory* "Visit by Video" service. This national clearinghouse of boarding school videos allows families or counselors to order by toll-free telephone line and credit card up to ten videos assembled on a single VHS cassette. For just $4 per selection, prospective applicants can pay a virtual visit to schools whose *Directory* write-ups seem to match their needs and interests. Each customized tape includes "Boarding Schools: The Video," a generic program extolling the excitement and opportunity of living where you learn. Developed by Boarding Schools in association with School Home Videos (1-800-248-7177), "Visit by Video" now offers over 60 school videos. From the other end, admission offices can fax the names of potential applicants to the Philadelphia-based company, which will send the school's video quicker than they could send it themselves.

Your choice of boarding school videos for just $4.00 per school

Visit by Video brings the campuses you've just read about to your living room. Although a video can't take the place of a real school visit, more and more families are using videos to begin the process of finding a school that will match their needs, interests and lifestyles.

To order your personalized selection of videos, simply choose the schools* from this *Directory* whose programs you wish to see and call 1-800-637-8308. For just $4 per school, chargeable to your Mastercard or Visa, we'll send you up to 10 videos conveniently recorded on a single VHS cassette.

And with every tape ordered, we'll include a free copy of "Boarding Schools: The Video." This 15 minute program documents the excitement and opportunity of living where you learn.

Boarding Schools' Visit by Video :
the next best thing to being there
To order, call 1-800-637-8308

This symbol ☐ at the end of a school listing indicates that the school participates in the Visit by Video service. This symbol ☐ denotes a school that has a video but prefers to send it directly to inquirers.

By whatever means, get the show out. The initial cost of a video may seem intimidating (though we repeat, it can pay for itself with a single extra admission). Yet once that outlay has been made, the extra expense for distribution is piddling. Reproduction of videos grows cheaper every year, and the mechanisms for disseminating them grow more refined. Cast the net wide! A good school video is a work of art, a reflection of the community that can build unity, instill pride and deepen loyalties; but its service can go much further in beckoning future generations to the unique school experience you know and cherish.

Tom Griffith, an expert on the use of video and slide-tape productions in enrollment marketing, is the author of The Audio-Visual Marketing Handbook for Independent Schools, *published in 1987 by Boarding Schools.*

Information Systems and Enrollment Management

DON SMITH

"I've been fat, and I've been thin, and I'll take fat any day."
— Dr. H. Conrad Warlick,
  Vice President for Administrative Services,
  Mary Washington College

Conrad Warlick's facetious perspective on enrollment management illuminates the most basic need for information systems. Today's admission officers are faced not only with the pressure to keep enrollments "fat," but must also devise marketing strategies that are more dependable and accountable than ever.

Information management and office automation are two very necessary parts of any fully integrated enrollment management approach. We spend handsomely for color view books, direct mail marketing, video production, and far flung recruitment efforts ranging from the neighboring zip code to the other side of the world. But how wise is it to produce a $35,000 video if your office automation system is so antiquated that you can't get a copy to a candidate promptly? How effective can the director of admission be in persuading the school head, or board, to fund a new advertising effort when she can't document the impact of the school's current ad campaign? How effective is an award winning view book if the letter accompanying it is poorly written, badly printed or only vaguely personalized? How can admission travel be effectively planned without precise knowledge of the location and status of current inquirers and most productive referral sources? It becomes quickly apparent then that information management and office automation are crucial aspects of independent school marketing and admission.

If an office of enrollment management is to be a powerful one, the director must use the resources of hardware, software, and "humanware" to reach the school's constituency. Planning must begin with the software needs of the enrollment management team. Too often schools purchase a hardware sys-

Figure A
Enrollment Management System Requirements

◆ *Separate Student/Candidate & Network Databases*

◆ *Ability to Store All Pertinent Candidate Information*

◆ *Ability to Cross-Reference Students and Referrers*

◆ *Automatic Selection for Correspondence*

◆ *Automatic Correspondence Management/Tracking*

◆ *Automatic Candidate Tracking/Updating*

◆ *Maintenance of Attending Student Database*

◆ *Automatic Generation of Statistical Reports*

◆ *Automatic Generation of Operational Reports*

◆ *Support for Mailings to Selected Students, Parents, & Referral Sources*

◆ *Support for Financial Aid Process*

◆ *Ability to Produce Highly Individualized Correspondence*

◆ *Ability to Create Complex Multi-Line Reports*

◆ *Support for Presentation Graphics*

◆ *Support for Interface to Spreadsheet*

◆ *Support for Database Audit and Automatic Repair*

◆ *Support for Interfaces to Registrar's and Other Systems*

tem only to find that the software they require will not operate reliably, or at all, on the hardware.

WHAT YOUR SOFTWARE SHOULD BE ABLE TO DO

Minimum software requirements for today's enrollment management office are listed above in figure A. Many of the seventeen minimum requirements outlined were probably obvious as you examined the figure. Some that are often overlooked are:

Referral sourcing: the ability to support, track, and cross-reference those people or leads that directed a candidate to the school.

It is critical to support educational consultants, the school's "network" of parents and alums, and advertising leads with an information system. The trap of communicating with, tracking, and reporting on only those people who inquire about the school is a deadly one. In fact, the most important people in the admission process are those who tell someone about that particular institution. Referral sources must be linked in the database to the candi-

dates they contacted who went on to inquire about the institution. As well, an information system must allow for the maintenance of different kinds of information on referrers as opposed to the type of information necessary to communicate with and measure the inquiry pool (see figure B). Thus, a separate referrer database is an absolute requirement for admission/marketing software.

Figure B

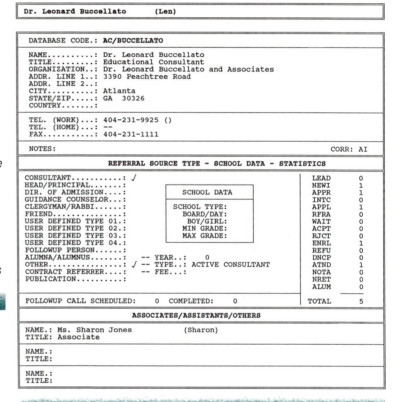

Report generation: the ability to easily create effective reports using any data available.

Systems that do not allow easy and significant report construction will not serve your long term needs. The director, associates, and administrative staff must be able to design reports that assist in travel planning, yield predictions at several stages of the admission process (see figure C), tracking of budget line items, cross-referencing referrers and the candidates they referred (see figure D), etc. Take a long, hard look at the report writing capabilities of any software solution. Be certain that the report writer is easy to use yet powerful and flexible, and that it will produce presentation quality reports.

Presentation graphics: support for presentation graphics and necessary interfaces.

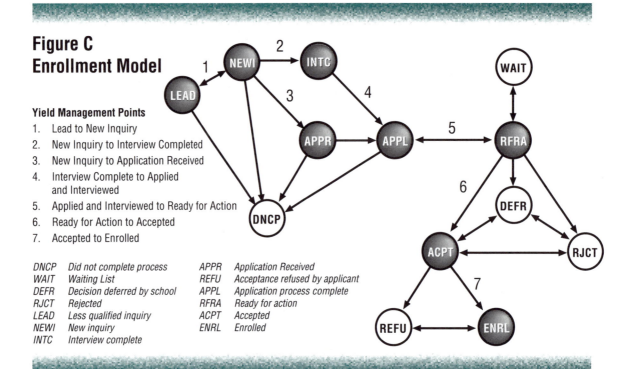

Figure C
Enrollment Model

Yield Management Points
1. Lead to New Inquiry
2. New Inquiry to Interview Completed
3. New Inquiry to Application Received
4. Interview Complete to Applied and Interviewed
5. Applied and Interviewed to Ready for Action
6. Ready for Action to Accepted
7. Accepted to Enrolled

DNCP	Did not complete process	APPR	Application Received
WAIT	Waiting List	REFU	Acceptance refused by applicant
DEFR	Decision deferred by school	APPL	Application process complete
RJCT	Rejected	RFRA	Ready for action
LEAD	Less qualified inquiry	ACPT	Accepted
NEWI	New inquiry	ENRL	Enrolled
INTC	Interview complete		

Figure D

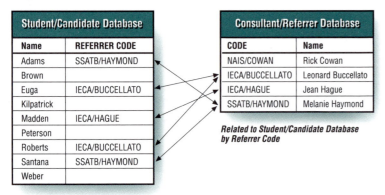

Student/Candidate Database

Name	REFERRER CODE
Adams	SSATB/HAYMOND
Brown	
Euga	IECA/BUCCELLATO
Kilpatrick	
Madden	IECA/HAGUE
Peterson	
Roberts	IECA/BUCCELLATO
Santana	SSATB/HAYMOND
Weber	

Related to Consultant/Referrer Database by Referrer Code

Consultant/Referrer Database

CODE	Name
NAIS/COWAN	Rick Cowan
IECA/BUCCELLATO	Leonard Buccellato
IECA/HAGUE	Jean Hague
SSATB/HAYMOND	Melanie Haymond

Related to Student/Candidate Database by Referrer Code

An important part of the admission "constituency" is the school's own board of directors. Admission officers are being held accountable for ever increasing budgets and staffs. Acceptable software will support the production of first rate presentations detailing how the admission budget and the time and energies of the staff are allocated. A graph depicting the results of the resources invested in an admissions weekend or day school reception will go a long way toward providing funds for a similar effort in the future. Boards don't expect something for nothing, they simply expect us to prove that our budget is being wisely utilized. Software is a critical tool in providing that evidence.

Interface ability: support for interface to registrars, business and development offices, and other systems.

A software solution must be able to export data in a wide variety of formats. This is not to say that the system must be a "fully integrated school system." In fact, the premise that all of an institution's software must be developed by the same group or look or feel like all the other software in the school is erroneous. It is far more important to have a local system that serves the important needs of admission and marketing than it is to have a program that looks or feels like a business or development program. Data gathered by the office of enrollment management must be able to be transferred to other offices in a variety of formats—that is the key to integration.

SYSTEM ACQUISITION

Having reviewed these minimum requirements for an admission/marketing system, put your particular needs at the very top of the list as you begin the process of system acquisition. System acquisition can be viewed as a nine step process. Figure E outlines the steps you might follow in buying hardware and software.

Regarding software, consider four alternatives for systems development.
- Develop a system internally
- Contract for a custom solution
- Buy a package
- Buy a state-of-the-art customizable package

Figure E
System Acquisition

- ◆ *Define Your Requirements*
- ◆ *Evaluate Alternatives*
- ◆ *Select Acquisition Strategy*
- ◆ *Justify Cost*
- ◆ *Plan Implementation*
- ◆ *Acquire System*
- ◆ *Install and Test*
- ◆ *Train Users and Directors*
- ◆ *Use the System*

From my perspective, the last of the four approaches makes the most sense. Although designing a system internally might seem the ideal alternative, I would caution against that strategy for two reasons. First, only one office is using the system for admission/marketing needs. This deprives the user of the opportunity to gather input from a user group regarding new and creative uses of the software. The importance of having a group of knowledgeable users cannot be overstated. Second, a system used only by one office cannot be as well tested and robust as a system in use in many settings. The single greatest problem facing users of internally developed systems is a program that crashes or is found inadequate after the user begins pushing the limits of the software. Either of these problems can be a dead end if the person who developed the system is no longer around to fix it or lacks the time or expertise to develop it further. Use caution in trying to develop a system internally.

The advantages of acquiring a customizable package are many. The system will be well tested and robust. The user is given the opportunity to influence the design of the system. The references of the system's developer can be checked to see if the system is continually upgraded and if it is well maintained. The cost will be considerably less than having a systems developer custom-design a solution. A user support group will be in place. An easy to use manual should be available. The system should meet all the needs designated at the very beginning of the systems acquisition process, or the vendor must be willing to customize the system to meet those requirements.

A fully usable software solution for admission/marketing needs should include:

1) an easy to use, fully developed user interface incorporating the latest software developments (graphical interface, "pop-up" lists for data input, speed function "hot" keys, etc.)
2) a pro-active database management system
3) a state-of-the-art word processor
4) a report writer capable of accessing multiple databases
5) a presentation quality graphics program
6) a professional spreadsheet program
7) an audit mechanism
8) a back-up mechanism

A vendor should present a fully integrated admission/marketing system and should be able to demonstrate the model upon which the system is based. Access to any one program from a command or menu screen is standard. A knowledge of DOS (see definition, p. 75) commands should not be necessary to operate the system, although the users should pursue training in the basics of DOS if they are not familiar with it.

NOTES OF CAUTION AND ENTHUSIASM

As you begin to shop for software, I sound one note of caution and another of enthusiasm. Be cautious of a "canned" program or a group of applications that are designed to meet a multitude of needs. Programs like Microsoft's Works or Wordperfect's group of Letterperfect, Planperfect, Dataperfect, etc. are interesting and noteworthy. However, they are "perfect" examples of programs loaded with compromises to make them serve a variety of uses. Programs of this type are in no way the answer to today's admission/marketing needs.

Software development is just now catching up with almost unbelievable hardware enhancements. Take advantage of the latest advances (such as windows applications, audit mechanisms, exciting user interfaces) that a customized program would offer. Don't allow your office to be "tempted into mediocrity" by using a less than state-of-the-art system. Getting the best is not that expensive, and is certainly cost-effective. In fact, if a vendor cannot give you concrete demonstrations of how their system can be used as a cost-effective solution, look elsewhere. Software designers have made dramatic progress in recent years, and promise to deliver even more impressive products in the near future. Look for greater capabilities in the allocation of memory, intuitive interfaces, and inexpensive networking so-

Portrait of an effective admission system

PROACTIVE DATABASE

It is important that the database management program be pro-active. By that I mean the system, not the user, should automatically move candidates through the admission process, based on the user's pre-defined criteria. The system should prompt the user to send appropriate letters based on the user's pre-defined time span, and the system should feature a "paper trail" mechanism that displays which correspondence has been sent, and prevents (automatically) the sending of repetitive letters. Nothing is worse than sending (or receiving) a highly personalized form letter—twice! The database system should automate the enrollment process, as opposed to the user being forced to move candidates through the system.

Figure C outlines the model upon which The Exeter Group's Enrollment Management System is based. This model allows the system to truly automate the candidate's movement through the admission process. Any effective software will do the same. The database system should also allow instant access to the data based on an almost endless number of or types of queries. An "account number" or other identifier should not be needed to view a candidate's record. Today's software can allow for an unlimited number of "user defined queries."

STRONG WORD PROCESSOR

A word processing system is not the place to save money or to use anything less than a top-of-the-line product. Even the very best are not terribly expensive anyway. Microsoft's Word 5.5 or Word for Windows and Wordperfect 5.1 are two examples of word processors that meet the needs of an admission office. Much of the daily work in an admission office is related to correspondence. Output must be of the highest quality, the database must allow correspondence to be highly personalized, and the word processing program must support significant merge capabilities.

AUDIT/FIX CAPABILITY

An audit/fix mechanism is an often overlooked but critically important part of a fully usable system. The audit mechanism must be built into the database system, and should audit data for common entry mistakes such as errors of omission. The system should automatically correct some mistakes, and it should prompt the user to fix records that it believes to be incorrect.

RELIABLE BACKUP

Lastly the system must include a highly reliable, fast, easy-to-use backup system. Hardware fails, and data is lost. A backup system that is slow or awkward to operate often discourages users from faithfully backing up their data. Murphy's law seems to apply here; inevitably the day (or week) you do not "back up" is the time a disk crashes. Take heed, be certain your software has a good backup mechanism. Fifth Generation System's Fastback Plus is one of many that are highly recommended, as is the Colorado Systems tape drive.

Figure F

The Next Marketing Handbook for Independent Schools

lutions. So shop around, look carefully, and dive in—the water's fine!

HARDWARE

Although the IBM vs. Apple computer debate looms large in the educational arena, this is not as big an issue in some other contexts. Since even within our independent school realm comparatively few Apple systems are used for significant database applications, I will focus on IBM and IBM clone hardware.

Software design and acquisition is the place to start defining information system and office automation needs. Having found (or developed) software that is appropriate for your needs, buy hardware that will run the software quickly and reliably. Hundreds of vendors produce highly reliable products ranging from "tower" 486 based file servers to the new generation of "notebook" computers. Many of these machines are offered through local representatives or through direct mail catalogs. Local vendors offer the assurance of a ready hand to assist you in matters of installation and maintenance. This assurance often comes at a premium, and many mail order companies (Dell Computer Corporation is one) have excellent service reputations. Prices for IBM compatible hardware are often excellent and there are many resources available to help you find which hardware is highly rated and which is not. An "editors choice" in one of the personal computer magazines is usually worth a second look.

PRINTERS

The automated office has seen extraordinary change in even the past five years. One of the most noteworthy of these changes has come in the area of hardware—the laser printer. By using a laser to fuse toner onto paper, this technology has changed the way printed matter looks today. Laser printers support a multitude of type styles and sizes, and operate quickly and almost silently. They print on standard paper, envelopes, labels, and transparencies. Hewlett Packard first introduced the laser printer and remains the leader in that technology today. Several companies have HP clones available at competitive prices. Laser printers range in price from less than $1,000 for "personal" laser printers to more than $5000 for top-of-the-line models. Laser printers are not well suited for printing "multi-part" forms: other than that singular application, there is really no reason to purchase any other type of printer.

ACCESSORIES

Beyond computers and printers, the hardware needs of the admission office may vary widely. Modems are helpful for accessing remote support for your software, for copying files from a remote computer to your office system, and for tapping into information services such as Compuserve and Prodigy. Many families have home computers linked to information services that provide you with an opportunity to communicate with them at home via on-line communication. Fax boards are arriving on the scene, and are receiving good reviews now that the initial models have been refined somewhat. A UPS (Uninterruptable Power Supply) is worth its weight in gold when the power goes off. A UPS will allow you time to exit your system and save data. Many companies now offer attractive hardware lease options as well as typical charge plans.

NETWORKS

A "networked" hardware/software solution allows an entire staff to share resources that were once available to only one user. If one computer has a printer, the other computers "on the network" can now use it. If one PC has a hard drive and the others have only floppy drives, they will each function as if they had a hard drive. Databases, and applications such as word processing, report writing, and graphics, can also be shared across the network.

The advantages of a networked system are many. A true "network" involves the linking of two or more devices (usually separate computers) over a cable, or even via a radio signal. Often the devices are "daisy chained" together by telephone or shielded cable designed specifically for the network hardware. There are a number of powerful network systems available and they range in price from less than a thousand dollars to several times that.

Many networks offer additional features such as disk caching (to increase the speed at which the file server operates) and even voice communication across the network.

It is here that the happy paradox of information systems emerges; by freeing us to do what we do best and prefer to do—communicate with families and respond creatively to marketing challenges—computers actually humanize our work.

The primary advantage of a network solution is access. Using a network to link the computers in the admission office will allow the director, associates, and support staff immediate and concurrent access to all of the data and related applications. Given this access, people learn how to use the applications much faster, make far greater use of the information available to them, and produce a higher standard of correspondence. Obviously, people beyond the admission office can also enter the system by "joining the network." Thus the need for some form of security. It is also wise to consider appointing someone to serve as a "network manager" if the network is very large or complex.

Networking a series of PCs is also a very cost-effective solution to information system and office automation needs. Because networking allows for the sharing of resources, substantial savings can be realized by not purchasing duplicate hardware. One printer can be shared by several users, less powerful (and less expensive) computers can act as workstations, served by one powerful (and more expensive) file server. Thus you gain the speed of a more powerful system, and access to its data storage capacity without the cost of expensive duplicate systems.

USING YOUR SYSTEM

Only your imagination limits the use of an information systems solution. Ours is used for a wide variety of tasks from writing, editing, and printing our daily correspondence to aiding us in planning our travel and advertising. I always travel with a portable PC, finding it invaluable to operate away from my office as effectively as I would seated at my desk at Cranbrook. Impressive portable printers are now available that further increase the efficiency of the "on the road" admission officer.

TRAINING

Everyone involved in the process of admission and marketing at your school should seek to become an expert user of the enrollment management software. Good software solutions are easy to use and, at the other extreme, provide the user with almost unlimited access to data and applications. Training programs should allow staff members to become effective users of the system for routine applications, and should bring about an understanding of the theory or model upon which the software is based. Only when the latter is understood should you expect to fully utilize the power of modern information and office automation systems. Be patient, as "expert" users are neither born nor created overnight. However, the learning curve of most applications is such that users move quickly from novice to more advanced use.

There is often some fear associated with moving toward an office automation system that is as inclusive as the model solution I am proposing. Administrative staff members who are unfamiliar with PCs might be hesitant to learn a new system, or to turn from their tried and true system to one that is less labor-intensive. Patience and excellent training are usually the answer to such an obstacle. Staff members should play some role in the design of the system and in its integration into their tasks. Since learning everything there is to know about a fully integrated system is an intimidating task, initially assigning specific duties to various members of the staff is wise. An example would be to have one person enter all new data and send initial correspondence, one person to update records and send letters of confirmation, and one person to become an expert user of the report writer. One staff member should be assigned the duties of backing up data daily and of running typical maintenance operations such as audit functions and hard disk maintenance. Allowing the staff to become comfortable with part of the system very quickly will give them more confidence when they tackle its more difficult aspects.

It is short-sighted to see a software system as a solution to any single problem. A successful solution will be both an effective information manager

> *Prior to the installation of our computer system, we spent nearly two weeks designing, writing and mailing our re-enrollment contracts. We used between 60 and 80 person-hours to complete that process. Our information system now allows us to produce and mail those same contracts (in a much more readable format) in less than one day. That's what I call a cost-effective solution.*
>
> — Robert J. Murphy, III
> Director of Admission,
> Christchurch School, VA

Don Smith is the director of admission at the Cranbrook Schools (MI). Previously, he was director of admission at Christchurch School (VA) where he developed the model upon which The Exeter Group's Enrollment Management System (EMS) is based. Don is a member of the SSATB's Annual Meeting Planning Committee, a past president of the Virginia Admissions Group, and an associate in the Cambridge, MA based firm of Charles J. Smith and Associates, a leading software development organization. An experienced educator and manager, he serves as enrollment management consultant for several NAIS schools.

and a system that saves an almost unbelievable amount of time on repetitive tasks. To adapt one of the catch phrases of the '90s, "use your system locally, but think how you might apply it globally."

HUMANWARE, WHERE HIGH TECH BECOMES "HIGH TOUCH"

Having explored hardware and software, we are left with the most complex component of the system, the one the editor of this book has dubbed "humanware."

It is here that the happy paradox of information systems emerges; by freeing us to do what we do best and prefer to do—communicate with families and respond creatively to marketing challenges—computers actually humanize our work. These high tech tools enable those of us who use them well to become "high touch" administrators.

The greatest contribution a good information system can make to your school is to give you and your staff more time to develop the context that independent education prides itself on—one on one communication between a caring, thoughtful adult and a young person.

Creative computing:

12 WAYS TO GET THE MOST OUT OF YOUR INFORMATION SYSTEM

1. Track the effectiveness of your display advertising, direct mail and alumni network programs with your database management program. Prove the cost effectiveness of specific programs to your board by tracking their results. Present the results in an attractive, easy to interpret graph or drawing.

2. Take a portable PC on the road with you. You will have access to your admission database while away, and you can send correspondence back to your office immediately (via modem), or simply print it when you return—either way your travel time is used more effectively.

3. Replace the weekly rummaging of the files with a report that lists any candidate who has applied and interviewed but is missing one or more pieces of required data. Design the report to print what is missing, what has been received, and any other necessary information. Put the candidate's home phone on the report and use it for a telephone list (see figure G).

4. Surprise your upper-school candidates by sending them an "electronically mailed" acceptance letter via Compuserve or Prodigy. The "techies" (and they wouldn't have the service if they weren't) will love it!

5. Use a word processor and desktop publishing program to publish an admissions newsletter for candidates, their families, and people in your network of referral sources.

6. Write user-defined queries to locate your constituency. "All candidates from Florida with SSAT's above the 60th percentile" might be an example.

7. Use a word processor with a database program to quickly print high-quality, personalized re-enrollment and enrollment contracts.

8. Spill your data into a spreadsheet/graphics program to highlight the most effective recruitment programs for your board and staff.

9. Use a word processor to automate the writing and printing of repetitive correspondence (new inquiry letters, some follow-up letters).

10. Use database management and calendar creator programs to produce an admission calendar, including the times and periods in which your campus guides are available.

11. Use a database program to append information into SSATB's MAPS system to give you valuable information about school choice factors for your inquiries, test-takers, applicants, and matriculants. Doing so would represent valuable market research at a fraction of the cost of most contracted research (see figure H).

12. Use a report writer to go beyond the typical "monthly" report to devise reports keyed to your admission season or special events. A report delineating the yield on interviews that included spring overnight visits would be interesting.

Figure H
Income Level Country Day Test Takers

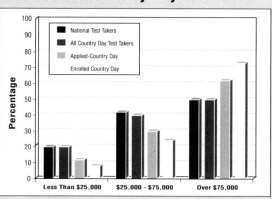

Figure G
Candidate Report

1.	ALGER, Summer Poole						STATUS	APP RCVD		
REQUIREMENT		APPL	ENGL	TCH1	PERS	WRIT	TRAN	TEST	OTH1	OTH2
RECEIVED = √		√	√	√	√	√	√	√	-	-

APPLYING FOR GRADE: 10-BRD-REG   INT. SCHED: Y 02-May-91
DATE OF LAST ACTION: 08-Mar-91   INT. COMPL: N
DAYS SINCE LAST ACTION: 51   SPECIAL PRG: ESL

REF: APP RECEIVED: 11/27/90
H/W: F/A REQUIRED: N

P1: Ms. Sue Scharth   TEL: (305) 338-2771
W1: (305) 244-6705   W2:

Glossary

ASCII (ASS kee) acronym for American Standard Code for Information Interchange. A standard seven-bit code, almost always transmitted with a parity bit (for a total of eight bits per character), that was established by the American National Standards Institute to achieve compatibility between various types of data processing and data communications equipment. ASCII is the most commonly used code for IBM PCs and other non-IBM equipment.

BIT (contraction of BINARY UNIT) a digit in the binary number system represented by a 0 or a 1. A bit is the smallest unit of storage in a computer.

BYTE a group of consecutive bits forming a unit of storage in a computer. A byte usually consists of eight bits.

CACHE (MEMORY) high speed memory used between the CPU and the main memory: cache memory is used to store sequences of instructions from the main memory. When the CPU needs an instruction, it first searches cache memory instead of the slower main memory. If the instruction is found in the cache memory, it is called a hit.

CANNED (PROGRAM) a program or group of programs which do not allow for user customization.

CPU acronym for Central Processing Unit. The part of a computer where operations are fetched, decoded, and executed, and the overall activity of the computer is controlled.

DOS (acronym for Disk Operating System) a program that controls all other applications, information storage, and the physical devices that constitute the computer.

FLOPPY DISK a disk, made of mylar, that can be magnetized to store information. Many computers contain one or more floppy disk drives. Floppy disks are usually either 5.25 or 3.5 inches in diameter. Floppy disks store approximately one megabyte of information.

HARD DISK a rigid disk, constructed of ceramic or aluminum and coated with a magnetic surface used to store data in the computer. Hard disks can store in excess of 100 megabytes of information.

KILOBYTE 1,024 bytes.

LAN (acronym for Local Area Network) a series of devices linked together for the purpose of shared resources.

LASER PRINTER a printer which operates by using a laser to fuse toner onto paper. Produces very high quality results quietly and quickly.

MEGABYTE one million bytes.

RAM (acronym for RANDOM ACCESS MEMORY) a type of memory in which any location can be accessed directly without having to follow a sequence of storage locations.

ROM (acronym for READ ONLY MEMORY) a type of memory chip that can be read but cannot be written on or altered. ROM provides permanent storage for program instructions.

SERVER (FILE) a powerful computer that "serves" files to other computers on a LAN.

VGA (acronym for Video Graphics Array) the minimum standard for video terminals in the enrollment management office. VGA monitors support high resolution (640 X 480) pixels and a dot-pitch of less than .28 mm. This monitor is necessary for high resolution, comfortable viewing, and high-quality graphics display. Color VGA monitors are becoming the standard. Consider SUPER VGA (1024 X 768 pixels) as well.

What Every School Head Should Know About Marketing

DREW CASERTANO

SCHOOL OF DREAMS?

"If you build it, he will come." So said a voice from the heavens to Ray Kinsella (Kevin Costner) in the wonderful film "Field of Dreams." Build it he did. Carved a jewel of a ballpark right out of some of his best Iowa cornfields. Most folks thought he was daffy. With good reason, since he darn near lost his farm. But Shoeless Joe Jackson came and brought other ballplayers with him — two full teams, in fact. And as the movie closes, we see the fans arriving — thousands of them. All with no encouragement (read marketing). All because Ray believed the voice.

Oh, if only it were so for independent schools. Build a gem of a school with superb teaching and a quality experience for each student and the applicants would come — in sufficient numbers — every year.

Today, that is nothing but a pipe dream. For most schools, marketing, outreach, recruitment — whatever phrase you find most palatable — is a necessity. And rather than think of it as a necessary evil (as in, the good schools really don't have to do it), we must embrace it as fundamental to institutional health with benefits reaching far beyond the obvious goal of expanding the applicant pool.

THE MAGIC OF THE MESSAGE

Good marketing, the kind that generates genuine interest in a school among prospective students and their parents, begins with the message; the words that accurately describe the essential qualities of a school. As both Bruce Buxton and Joy Sawyer Mulligan write in their excellent chapters, effective marketing "begins at home." Thus, the message must be grounded in what the school is or will quickly become. More specifically, with input from a school's many constituencies and an understanding of its myths, stories and history, it is the head's responsibility to develop that message, monitor its accuracy and see to it that it is shared in countless ways. After all, the strength and appeal of our

more generally, how do families act when considering an independent school education for their son or daughter?

Through the Marketing Analysis Profile (MAP) and Promoting Independent Education (PIE), SSATB and NAIS have given us very useful responses to these questions and more. You can obtain additional, equally valuable information simply by asking good questions. And listening.

We must embrace marketing as fundamental to institutional health with benefits reaching far beyond the obvious goal of expanding the applicant pool.

MAKING THE TEAM

Effective marketing also requires team work. To be sure, the admissions and development offices, and other areas, such as college counseling in a secondary school, play lead roles in the process. But so many others are involved. This is especially evident if you regard enrollment management — the retention of our current students and enrollment of new ones to reach an appropriate size student body — as intrinsic to good marketing. Here, again, the head's responsibility begins with understanding, this time of the merits of team work. He or she must develop a cooperation among everyone at school and particularly those groups which have the most contact with the world outside our doors. Several examples come to mind: the content, appearance and schedule of mailings to our parents; the clarity of information shared with newly enrolled families; the appearance of enrollment contracts and our billing statements, especially as the figures which they contain grow increasingly substantial; teachers' comments and other communication with parents about their child's performance; any contact that the school has with outside groups (including its signs for visitors) for that matter. We pay careful attention (not to mention great sums of money) for our viewbooks and alumni magazines, but are we cognizant of the message being conveyed by these other forms of communication? We simply can't afford not to be. This awareness begins with the head and must become part of a school's culture.

schools stems primarily from our ability to define our respective missions and then fulfill them. For the head, this is where marketing must begin.

You must understand that whether conciously our not, each school sends powerful messages about itself. Is there any debate about the advantage of our knowing just what those messages are and our having some control over them by sending clear, accurate and appealing signals about who we are? If those messages can't be positive, then here, too, the head has some serious work to do.

LEARNING TO LISTEN, LISTENING TO LEARN

In Chapter 13 Bill Cole extols the value of listening to your students, teachers, graduates, applicants. Listening to as many individuals involved with the school as possible is essential to successful marketing. By thus providing feedback from a variety of sources, effective marketing generates information, as well as increased interest in the school. As such, it is an extremely valuable tool for school heads as they lead and seek to improve their schools.

Not surprisingly, listening well begins with asking good questions. Or to phrase it another way, in marketing, common sense is worth more than all the consultants, designers and producers available. Before thinking about target populations, focus groups, visibility studies or other forms of "marketing speak," consider who your students are. What brought them to the school? What will continue to attract similar types of families? Who else do you want to attract? What will have that effect? Or,

THE HEAD–ADMISSION OFFICER RELATIONSHIP

There comes, as well, the need for a school head to understand the pressures that admission officers face today. Simply put, it is grueling work. As expectations have risen and the climate for independent schools has become less favorable, admission officers have found themselves running faster and faster to stay in place. If this continues, it is a legitimate worry that fewer individuals will see themselves capable of sustaining this pace and fewer yet will find themselves attracted to the profession in the first place. Both outcomes can only have a damaging effect on our schools.

Heads can help tremendously by sharing clear expectations with the admission staff and by giving them the opportunity to participate in goal-setting.

This begins with enrollment goals and an understanding of the types of students best served by a school. It is equally important that efforts be made to resist the isolation that can easily overcome an admissions staff. They must be part of an information loop that enables them to share reactions from outside constituencies, have input into the setting of policies that shape the daily experiences that they represent, and receive feedback from their faculty and colleagues, and, of course, the head about the perceptions of the school and the students they have enrolled.

THE HEAD–TRUSTEE RELATIONSHIP

The head's relationship to the trustees plays a further role in marketing. This involves working with board members to determine what information about campus activity will be most useful to them as they fulfill their role as broad policy makers. Equally important, they must have the opportunity to inform themselves of and discuss the "megatrends" that are sure to affect all schools as we approach the new millenium. Only with an understanding of the forces and issues at work will they muster the creativity needed to respond to the range of vexing problems facing our schools. Among the most challenging of those problems is affordability, an issue that requires the utmost cooperation between board and head.

MORE THAN SALESMANSHIP

From a head's perspective, good marketing is much more than effective salesmanship. It requires the cooperation, clear expectations, exchange of information and definition of purpose that can and should play a prominent role in the dynamic nature and daily lives of independent schools.

Drew Casertano became the sixth headmaster of Millbrook School (NY) in 1990. Previously, he served as director of admission and financial aid at the Loomis Chaffee School (CT) and The Gunnery (CT). Drew is a director of the Secondary School Admission Test Board and a graduate of Choate Rosemary Hall (CT).

Managing Admission's Multiple Priorities

BILL COLE

FAILURE BY DESIGN?

Many admission offices these days are set up to fail or, perhaps more accurately, to make the admissions director feel like a failure. Demands of interviewing, writing up interviews, office management, school committees, not to mention teaching, coaching, dormitory, and chaperoning responsibilities, make it nearly impossible to do the kind of planning upon which marketing depends. The first step to making marketing manageable is the hardest: negotiating with your head of school and with your board to give yourself three gifts—time, money, and information.

GIVE YOURSELF THE GIFT OF TIME

What reorganization of your office or redelegation of duties would allow you to set aside, say, every other Thursday from 10:00 until noon for planning and research? What would it take to set aside a week of your office's slowest season to design a three- to five-year marketing plan?

The press of calls to return, files to read, recruiting trips to schedule, and families to interview can deprive you of the time to step back, get perspective, and develop a long-range plan. For some directors, this same press actually serves as a convenient excuse for not planning: the everyday jobs are not only more pressing, they're easier, or at least more familiar.

Take a moment now to carve out marketing planning time on your calendar. Force yourself to keep to your schedule. Consider hiring consultants to work with you during some of these scheduled planning sessions. As Whitney Ransome points out in Chapter 15, consultants are valuable not just for the ideas they offer but also for their qualities as a sounding board for your own ideas. If consultants are working with you, your attention can't be diverted to more quotidian affairs—and you can develop a plan that will serve you and your school well for a long time. Lists of marketing consultants are available from NAIS's Department of Administrative Services

(617-451-2444) and Peterson's Guides, Inc. (800-338-3282).

GIVE YOURSELF THE GIFT OF MONEY

Schools historically have underfunded admissions and marketing—hence the straits schools face in recruiting today. Your office is responsible for bringing in at least 80% of your school's operating budget, depending on how much income is derived

What would it take to set aside a week of your office's slowest season to design a three- to five-year marketing plan?

from endowment, annual giving and other revenue sources such as summer camps and facility rental. What percentage of these tuitions is budgeted for your office expenses and for marketing?

The corporate model is useful here. Corporations typically budget 7% to 12% of their operating costs for advertising and marketing, more if it's a new product or service, less if it's well niched and needs little support.

If you were to calculate your total office expenses including salaries, travel, advertising, publications, phones, and so forth, what percentage of your school's operating budget would that constitute? It may be impossible to do the kind of outreach expected of you with the dollars your office is given by the board.

Even in these lean times it's important, too, to give yourself some "play" money. Set aside a fraction of your marketing budget for trying out new media: a postcard campaign like those at Girls' Prep (TN) or MacDuffie (MA), a new search piece, a display ad campaign in a different local newspaper, a recruitment trip to a "new" city, or a marketing campaign focusing on alumni of child-rearing age.

Not only do such hunch-based experiments often work, they nearly always teach you something. A director whose direct-mail campaign failed to produce a single enrollment told me that as a result of doing it she learned how to present information about her school and financial aid to new families much more effectively.

GIVE YOURSELF THE GIFT OF INFORMATION

The more you know about your school's constituencies and the more accurately you can read be-

tween the lines of this information, the more likely you'll make the right marketing decisions. Here are some questions you should try to answer:

◆ Where do my applicants live?

◆ Where do my enrollments and current students live? Is there a difference?

◆ How can I profile where these three groups live:
  - size?
  - type of community?
  - relative affluence of community?
  - types of schools available?
  - presence or absence of competitor schools?

◆ What similar cities, towns, or neighborhoods would be useful places to target marketing and recruitment travel?

◆ Where are the pockets of alumni/ae and current parent support that can help the admissions office?

◆ What is my cost per lead and cost per enrollment of each of the media—including recruitment travel—I use in my admissions outreach?

Increasing your office budget alone is not enough; it's important to spend your budget wisely. You need to develop the mechanisms to track your inquiries and enrollments and calculate the amount you spend for each. Asking both parents and kids for the sources of their knowledge about your school—and frequently there are several—will help you define the most effective means of marketing and the most efficient use of your marketing dollar.

Once you begin to get the time you need for planning, a budget appropriate to the task, and the information you need about your school's constituencies, you can begin to use the most important tool of marketing, one that can improve more radically your chances for success than any other—listening.

LEARNING TO LISTEN

Marketing is frequently compared to sales, because we all know what sales is, and maybe their ends are the same, but their means are quite different. If sales is talking, marketing is listening. Or put another way, sales is talking at, marketing is talking with. Put still another way, sales is saying what you think they want to hear; marketing is hearing what they need to say.

It's not that admissions doesn't involve both sales and marketing; it does. Your brochures and videos speak, and so, of course, will you, to "sell" your school. This part of the admission job is well known and a lot of time, money, and attention are focused on it.

The Next Marketing Handbook for Independent Schools

Good marketing, however, is often overlooked. Good marketing first involves asking the right questions and then listening and listening long and well. Good listening can radically alter your school and the way it presents itself to prospective students and their parents.

LISTEN TO THE STUDENT FIRST

The most important listening is listening to the kid first. Listening for his or her unspoken questions: Will I fit in here? Will the other kids like me? Will I do OK here? How will I handle (in the case of boarding schools) being separated from my family and friends? What can the school do to ease the admissions process? What can be done to make the transition into school more successful?

LISTEN TO THE PARENTS

Again, the unspoken concerns are the ones to listen most carefully for: Will my kid fit in here? Is this the best option for my child? Can we afford it? Is it safe? Is there transportation?

LISTEN TO YOUR CONSTITUENCIES

There are also the antennae admission directors need to have about the perception of their schools in the community and in comparison to other, similar schools. Market research is a great way to get fundamental questions about the school asked and their answers put into practice.

To thrive, independent schools must be a stand for quality in education. Compared to the bureaucracy that reigns in many public systems, a private school should be one that is easily correctable when there are flaws in quality. Translating what you hear into action plans with the head of school or board of directors to improve facilities, change personnel, or rethink a policy is an important part of your job. Not confronting and resolving problems that could jeopardize the school can sabotage the best sales and marketing.

MAKE IT EASY

Most parents of your prospective students both work these days. The times they will find it easiest to call you for information or to arrange interviews will be before and after work and during lunch. Make it easy on them. Arrange to have your phones answered from 8:00 am until 5:30 pm and during lunch.

Schools should get together and have a joint application form. I don't mean the essay questions, I mean the basics. Why should people have to fill out the most rudimentary information five or six times? Their time is valuable. Let's show we respect it.

How about putting application fees on charge cards to avoid check writing? It works for L.L. Bean. Or an 800-number for any and all school brochures? One call gets all.

LISTEN TO THE LANDSCAPE

Kids have to pass only the SSAT. Parents have to pass three very trying tests starting with the NFTDS—"Now Find The Damn School." NFTDS is often a result of there being little or no correlation between the admission brochure and a local map. There seems to be an inverse relationship between the fee we pay graphic designers for admissions maps and the clarity of the final product. I confess to having done this myself. A parent who was late for an interview held up my brochure map—which I thought was perfectly gorgeous—and asked, "Is this a map or a Mondrian?"

This first test is quickly succeeded by the NWBHAO—"Now Where in Bloody Hell is the Admission Office?" Is there signage directing families to your office? Are there marked spaces for admissions visitors?

Of course the ultimate exam is the WIGNITMR, "Where In God's Name Is The Men's Room?" Although most of the buildings housing admission offices were initially designed for something else completely, why must we steadfastly conceal the restrooms? Why must this be the first question an admissions officer or secretary has to handle?

LISTEN TO YOUR WAITING ROOM

Are your sofas comfortable or do men have to look at their knees when they sit down? What do you have for parents and kids to read while they're waiting besides old yearbooks and alumni/ae magazines? And how greasy are those yearbook pages? Anything to indicate that the school's interested in something beyond selling itself to parents? Something like *A Place Called School,* or one of Ted Sizer's books?

Can parents get a feeling for the school from the office? Are tea, coffee, water, and real (and

clean) china at hand? Is it comforting and welcoming? When Disney's Michael Eisner was setting up Touchstone Films, his watchwords were, "No snow, no rural." If I were setting up an admission office, mine would be, "No green, no linoleum."

MARKETING BEGINS AT HOME

The modes of listening described above are just the beginning. As Joy Sawyer Mulligan points out in Chapter 5, the most powerful marketing starts on your own campus. To the degree that you're successful with internal marketing, the rest of what I have to say may become irrelevant. Consider every aspect of your school's life—from student behavior during school events to report cards to college counseling to Parents' Weekend.

For example, food is critical to a school's morale, particularly a boarding school's. The most successful school food service I know actually weighs the amount of waste after each meal and rotates the least successful one off the menu each week. That's great listening.

LISTEN TO THE BIG BOYS

When you're getting yourself ready for marketing, read *Business Week, Inc.*, and brochures for Mercedes Benz, rather than school brochures. Large corporations and the publications that serve them spend a lot of money planning the presentation and articulation of a product. Unfortunately, school publications are often filled with recycled ideas. For the most part, reading them is like driving and looking in the rearview mirror. It's necessary to do sometimes, but looking out the windshield is much more productive.

FAVOR FACTS (AND ESCHEW CLAIMS)

I nearly always feel like *Dragnet's* Jack Webb when I read school brochures. I keep wanting to say, "Just the facts, ma'am." The most important feeling any communication from a school should elicit from a parent and a child is trust. Too often, however, the distinction between what's factual and what's merely a claim is blurred.

Instead of describing your "warm and caring faculty" for the umpteenth time, why not document a day in the life of one of your teachers?

> "10:00 to 10:45, taught Algebra I. 10:46 to 10:52 worked with Michelle Harding on equations. 10:53 to 10:56 checked with advisee Mike Richards about making up an essay for English. 2:45, met with JV tennis team..."

Such facts are infinitely more reassuring than claims. They create trust, the most important element you're trying to communicate. If you have to make claims, let photographs do the talking. Or let others make claims for you: quote current or past parents, or alumni/ae.

PURPOSE VS. RESULT

The wise manager of school marketing will always put the needs of the child and the family before those of the school. The distinction here is between purpose and result, two words whose meanings are often confused. If it is your purpose as admission director to do the best thing for the child, the result will be that the school is also best served…and that is marketing at its best!

Bill Cole is the director of school and camp services at Peterson's, Inc. He cut his teeth on marketing when teaching Latin at St. Albans School (DC) in the early 1970s to students more interested in the Grateful Dead. At the Madeira School (VA) Bill was director of student activities, assistant director of development, and director of Camp Greenway. He has spoken on marketing issues at conferences sponsored by The Council for the Advancement and Support of Education, the American Camping Association, NAIS, and the Secondary School Admission Test Board.

Where the kids are

Every August *Sales and Marketing Management* publishes a useful list of the top 320 or so metro and suburban areas in this country ranked by the number of children age 6-17 and the relative wealth of those areas. Overlaying this information with data about your own constituencies can offer vital clues as to what areas would be promising to target for marketing and travel. *Sales and Marketing Management,* 633 3rd Ave., NY, NY 10017 (212-986-4800).

CHAPTER 14: VIEW FROM THE BOARDROOM

The Trustee's Role in Marketing

RICK DALTON

CONTRASTING CASES

Blanchard Academy's enrollment drops from 320 to 280 students in one year. In a frantic meeting, the board considers these options:
a. Hiring a consultant;
b. Firing the admissions director;
c. Forming a marketing committee;
d. Appropriating $50,000 for marketing;
e. All of the above.

In its panic, the board gives the last choice greatest consideration. Two-thirds of the meeting is devoted to enrollment and admissions issues.

In contrast, OakRiver Country Day continues to enjoy a healthy admissions picture. In the last five years, the school's enrollment and the distribution of students from kindergarten through grade 12 has not fluctuated. Except for a cursory report every other meeting, the board rarely discusses admissions and enrollment issues.

Blanchard and OakRiver, both fictional schools, represent two ends of the continuum in the way boards treat marketing. Many boards either ignore marketing or overreact by "throwing wads of money at the problem," using everything from "helium balloons to TV spot ads," says Gregory Floyd, vice president of Browning Associates.

Although these schools face different situations, both need a strategic marketing plan. In Blanchard's case, such a plan will guide the school through its immediate crisis and enable it to make the right marketing decisions. OakRiver can use its marketing plan to chart future enrollment trends and prepare for any possible problems.

MARKETING IS HERE TO STAY

Enrollment marketing is no longer a foreign concept to independent schools. In fact, it has become a crucial tool in today's educational marketplace. School boards need to learn what role marketing plays in their admission and enrollment strategies. Many independent school leaders are

seeing that a well developed marketing plan can enhance admission by helping their school find and attract the students and families that best understand and appreciate the school.

PLANNING YOUR WAY THROUGH THE MARKETING MAZE

The board can begin by helping the admissions director and school head develop or revise a strategic marketing plan. This role ensures that marketing enables your school to meet its institutional goals and objectives rather than deplete resources. Without clear strategies, schools will wander aimlessly through the marketing maze.

THE FOUR KEY QUESTIONS

The four basic strategic planning questions boards need to address are: 1. Where are we? 2. Where do we want to go? 3. What factors influence our ability to get there? 4. How do we get there?

1) Where are we? This question establishes a context for the strategic marketing plan. As a board member, you must make sure that your school assesses its admissions and enrollment status. Good data provide a compass and allow you to chart your answer. If your school's enrollment or applications are down 12 percent, for example, you need to determine where this drop has taken place. Is the softening across all grades, only in the upper school, or just in tenth grade girls?

2) Where do we want to go from here? Once you assess enrollment status, you may decide that you want to stabilize enrollment at its current level or increase enrollment to some previous figure. Then the

board can establish marketing and enrollment goals and objectives, such as increasing enrollment by adding ten students in each of the upper school grades.

3) What factors influence our ability to get there? Answering this question means identifying internal and external factors that will either impede or enhance your ability to reach established enrollment and admissions goals. One approach, which also makes a good board exercise, is to list internal strengths and weaknesses and then external opportunities and threats (SWOT). When you identify internal weaknesses, you may determine that inadequate resources or poor communication impede enrollment gains. And the external threats may include poor public transportation and a sluggish local economy.

4) How do we get there? After answering the first three questions, you are now ready to create a marketing plan. The thrust of the marketing plan will be to eliminate and lessen the effect of identified weaknesses and threats. The plan may entail a school-supported busing program, a campaign to clarify image or the hiring of an additional admissions professional.

FINANCIAL AID AS A MARKETING TOOL

Financial aid is an essential component of marketing. It is likely to be one of your board's answers to question four and should be part of every school's marketing plan. Stable enrollments depend on strategically developed financial aid plans.

In the last few years, financial aid has consumed an increasingly larger portion of schools' overall budgets. One board member of a New England boarding school described financial aid as "the burr in the budgetary saddle." In just ten years, the average independent school has increased its aid budget by 260 percent, yet increased the number of students served by that aid by only 12 percent. The pool of families that can pay the full cost of an independent school education is shrinking. (See PIE Briefing #2 in this handbook's *Databank*.)

David Erdmann, a director of the Essex Institute for Enrollment Planning, has developed fiscal projections for schools that indicate financial aid budgets will need to double in ten years just to serve the same number of students. To stabilize enrollments, schools will be compelled to increase dollars spent on aid.

Many schools are caught in a conundrum: how can they stay fiscally sound and still maintain diversity by attracting both first generation independent school families and other groups that often cannot pay full cost (PIE Briefing #4).

The Next Marketing Handbook for Independent Schools

Many boards have responded to swelling aid expenditures by simply issuing the decree: no more aid! Other boards, because they have no plan, have been caught in a downward spiral of buying students to fill desks.

Keep in mind that financial aid is a marketing tool. Recent studies show that families unfamiliar with independent schools do not know about the availability of financial aid. Many of these families think independent schools are too expensive, yet they underestimate tuitions by an average of $2,000. Schools will need financial aid to bring new families into the pool. There will be an even greater need to use financial aid productively and prudently in the near future.

THE CHALLENGE OF METABOLIZING COMMERCIAL MARKETING EXPERIENCE

Trustees with marketing experience outside of education can be both a blessing and a curse. Schools can learn much from how marketing is used in other businesses; positioning, targeting, assessment are all principles that schools can apply to their marketing efforts. On the other hand, comparisons between tangible and intangible products are dangerous, as Rick Cowan notes in Chapter 1. One exasperated school head recently described the approach advocated by a marketer on his board: "He wants us to market the school as if we're selling hair brushes. That sort of marketing doesn't work for us." When questions arise about the applicability of an approach, turn to the strategic marketing plan for direction.

ESTABLISHING A MARKETING TASK FORCE

Perhaps the best way for trustees to contribute to a school's marketing effort is through a marketing task force. Schools need to harness their collective marketing wisdom and energy. Task forces can advocate the need for marketing, help create and review the marketing plan, measure its effectiveness and recommend effective marketing strategies. The composition of the task force should include those trustees with an interest in and knowledge of marketing, as well as those school leaders charged with implementing the policy: admissions, public relations, and development directors.

AVOIDING PANIC BUTTONS AND QUICK FIXES

Above all else, don't push the Panic Button: Tales abound of schools wasting marketing dollars on enrollment problems. One school with an enrollment shortfall of 35 students placed two dynamic, young classroom teachers on the road to recruit prospective students. Without proper training and guidance (and no strategic marketing plan!) the teachers floundered. The next year enrollment dropped again, and the two teachers, frustrated by the apparent futility of their efforts, left the profession. Another struggling school saw international markets as a panacea; Pacific Rim travel and related expenditures doubled their recruitment cost per stu-

Without clear strategies, schools will wander aimlessly through the marketing maze.

dent and created a host of other problems.

There are no quick fixes that will solve enrollment instability. When times are tough, go back to the four basic questions, and let the answers provide the framework of a renewed marketing plan. Glossier and slicker promotion does not create a healthier enrollment. It may be that the school's mission rather than its marketing campaign needs to be resolved first. Above all else, don't make the mistake of the Blanchard Academy board and react without the guidance of a strategic marketing plan.

A CRUCIAL CONTRIBUTION

Marketing, as the many authors of this book illustrate, is a prime concern of the independent school in the 1990s. It is as important to a school as hiring practices , alumni relations, and fund-raising. Board members with the ability and willingness to make marketing work for rather than against their school can make a crucial contribution to the institution whose future depends on their wisdom.

Rick Dalton is a trustee and an alumnus of The South Kent School (CT). After 10 years as director of enrollment planning at Middlebury College in Vermont, he left to become the executive director of the Foundation for Excellent Schools in 1991. Rick holds an Ed.D. from the Harvard Graduate School of Education, where he wrote his dissertation on enrollment management. A director of Essex Associates, a comprehensive enrollment consultancy group, Rick lectures often on market research, admission office management, and marketing.

CHAPTER 15: WHY GO IT ALONE?

Working With a Marketing Consultant

WHITNEY RANSOME

PARTNERS IN PROBLEM SOLVING

School leaders face an ever broadening range of management challenges. Most heads have recognized the importance of mission-based marketing, have staff members with marketing talent, understand the power of effective communications, and do an admirable job of pulling it all together. Yet what school hasn't wondered about its image? Wished that attrition were lower? Felt the need for a better catalog? Struggled to identify the marketing priorities? Awarded financial aid but pondered its efficacy? Knew its long term goals but wondered how to achieve them?

Complex tasks require many minds, many hands, and many hearts. Knowing when and how to seek specialized advice is a hallmark of the wise individual and the wise institution. An experienced consultant, armed with broad knowledge and experience, can be the objective partner who will help you reach your goals. Outside consultants can bring fresh wisdom to a school's challenges and possibilities. The best advisors are astute enablers who work with us, not for us. A good consultancy is a good partnership.

SELECTING A CONSULTANT: A HIRING ROADMAP

As with all hiring, the selection of an effective consultant requires thought, sensitivity, hard work and planning. Although the needs of schools will vary, the process of selecting a consultant can be simplified by a hiring roadmap.

1) Define the objectives and scope of your project. What is the school trying to accomplish? A better understanding of its image? A solution to high attrition? A comprehensive communications program? A school-wide enrollment management approach? Identification of new markets? Better relationships with school constituencies? Whatever the issue, the school needs to describe both the challenge and the desired outcome.

Navigating the marketing maze: why and how consultants can help

Consultants offer skills and perspectives that can be invaluable to a school as it navigates the marketing maze. While every school may not need or want a consultant, the following advantages should be considered when deciding whether or not to seek outside help.

SPECIALIZED EXPERTISE

Tasks such as these call for expertises rarely available in-house:

- Mission analysis
- Long-range planning
- In-depth market research
- Information systems development
- Video and viewbook production
- Professional public relations

Even the most competent of school people can learn something new from a professional with a specialized focus in one of these areas.

BROAD AND OBJECTIVE PERSPECTIVE

Someone outside an organization's hierarchy is often better able to identify and understand marketing issues. An experienced analyst can listen to different points of view within a school, distill the messages into recurring themes, and offer a reasoned yet new strategy. Consultants carry with them an awareness of a larger educational landscape. They understand national trends, demographics, technologies, and methodologies that could affect your school. A good consultant also appreciates the unique qualities of each institution and responds accordingly.

CLARITY OF VISION

In planning its future, a school must consider its history and traditions as well as its goals and dreams. That future is often best described by a third party practiced in both listening and consensus building. Many schools with superb programs, dedicated faculty, and happy families have somehow lost sight of how best to share that with the world beyond their campus. A consultant can help a school realize the important links among mission, program and marketing.

NEUTRALITY

A good consultant must, by definition, have no vested interest in one course of action versus another. The consultant's major role is to highlight what is best for the school, not what is in the interest of a particular individual.

CATALYST FOR ACTION

Successful marketing efforts must have definitive goals and deadlines. Consultants can help establish priorities and suggest appropriate courses of action. As an outsider, the consultant is better able to keep people on track. Unencumbered by internal school politics or day to day responsibilities, the consultant can infuse others with the energy and enthusiasm for long overdue or overlooked marketing tasks. Sometimes it is such renewed commitment from administrators, trustees, faculty, and parents that enables a school to reach important goals.

Further benefits of hiring an experienced consultant

- Knows what is and isn't likely to work, based on experience with other schools.
- Can reduce the time it takes to plan and implement a project.
- Can identify the best production resources.
- Can negotiate contracts.
- Can impart skills or design systems to increase staff self-sufficiency. A good consultant works to make her or himself unnecessary.
- May be able to cut through the politics of a particular institution.

2) **Establish a project advisory committee.** This committee will:
- identify possible consultants,
- review the candidates' qualifications,
- make the final choice,
- serve as the coordinating group for the project,
- act as liaison to the consultant.

Thought should be given to the composition of the group. Should it consist solely of administrators or should it include representatives from the trustees, faculty, parents, and student body?

Knowing when and how to seek specialized advice is a hallmark of the wise individual and the wise institution.

3) **Assemble names of consultants with appropriate credentials for the project under consideration.** NAIS's Consultant Referral Service is one of the best but not the sole source of names. The Secondary School Admissions Test Board (SSATB) and state and regional independent school organizations can also provide information about consultants. Talk with contacts at other schools. Undoubtedly, colleagues from similar institutions have solicited outside help and can describe the strengths and weaknesses of different advisers.

4) **Contact the consultants who seem most desirable.** Provide a verbal, followed by a written, description of the project goals and desired outcomes. Request a proposal that details how the consultant would handle the project. Ask for an estimate of how long it will take to complete the project, cost ranges and a references list. Give the consultants some basic information about the school (mission statement, catalog, video, long-range plan, recent admission statistics and market research) so they have a sense of your institution's mission and character.

5) **Choose a group of finalists for interviews.** Review the proposals and make preliminary reference calls to narrow the field. Select those consultants who seem most qualified for your job. Schedule interviews with the finalists and explore questions relating to background, previous experience, knowledge of subject, project methodologies, end products, expected schedule, and anticipated costs. Spend several minutes at the conclusion of the interview to discuss impressions. Establish the pros and cons of hiring each consultant. Have a member of the committee record the group's deliberations,

noting areas of consensus and disagreement.

6) **Check references.** Review the lists provided by the consultants and contact people who are familiar with the consultants' work. Questions to ask include: How was the consultant used? Did the consultant have a good understanding of the school? Did school personnel have easy access to the consultant? Were the tasks completed in a timely fashion? Was the consultant able to work effectively with different constituencies? Was the consultant flexible when necessary? Were the observations and recommendations offered helpful? Was the school better off after the consultancy? Were there any problems? Was the consultant available for ongoing advice as ideas were implemented?

7) **Evaluate the trust/comfort factor.** As with any successful relationship, there must be a high level of trust, confidence and comfort between school and consultant. Some questions to ponder:
- Does the consultant seem like a good match with the project and the personalities of your school?
- Can you imagine this person representing your school? What kind of first impression will he or she make? How credible is he or she?
- How good are the consultant's writing and speaking abilities?
- Does she or he truly understand independent schools?

8) **Draw up a letter of agreement with the consultant.** Once the choice has been made reiterate the goals, objectives, timetable and budget for the project. Prepare a letter of agreement that will be reviewed by the consultant. Incorporate any changes in the project that may have occurred since the original proposal was submitted. A jointly signed letter of agreement assures that the school and the consultant have the same understanding about what is expected of the consultancy.

9) **Thoroughly inform the consultant about your school and vice versa.** Most consultants will want a variety of materials in advance of a campus visit. They will also need to talk with representatives of the school's different constituencies. An explanatory memo sent to appropriate audiences at the school will help set the stage for the consultant's work. Explain why the consultant was hired, review the schedule he or she will have when on campus (class visits? individual and group interviews—random, handpicked or representative?) and how the visit relates to the overall project. Candor is important if the consultant is to do the job well, so urge full cooperation. Assure people that conversations

The Next Marketing Handbook for Independent Schools

The Consultant File*

WHY USE A CONSULTANT?

- Is institutional change needed to develop marketing expertise?
- Do head and/or board support marketing efforts suggested by the admission office or administrative team?
- Is your pool of qualified applicants shrinking?
- Do you possess sufficient marketing skills? If not, do you have the time/energy to develop them?
- Do you need reality testing? Is there a gap between your self-perception and the public view of your school?
- Are you truly receptive to outside ideas? If not, don't hire a consultant.

ADVANTAGES OF CONSULTANT OVER IN-HOUSE APPROACH

- Objective outside perspective. Not constrained by interest in maintaining internal relationships.
- Recommendations carry clout of an outside professional: useful in moving board and staff to fund and implement needed programs.
- Doesn't further burden overworked/understaffed middle management.

"Organizations using quality consultants prove to be more productive and ultimately more cost-effective."

— Tom Hodgkins
President, Lake Forest Academy
Former consultant, Booz, Allen, Hamilton

PITFALLS/DANGERS/DIFFICULTIES

- Don't pay a consultant to learn your business.
- Fear of firing; certain consultants have "ax man" reputation.
- Recognize the "buts" every consultant client must face:
  - "But our school is different..."
  - "But the consultant didn't talk to everyone..."
  - "But that won't work here"
  - "But the consultant doesn't really understand our school..."

Those "buts" may be true, *but* that's the point; consulting works best because it doesn't excuse the preservation of the status quo.

EXPECT THAT S/HE:

- will unsettle faculty and administration.
- will bother and divert your staff from daily tasks.
- cannot fix a crisis or repair deep-seated problems.
- will make mistakes.

"The perception of self-uniqueness is highly developed in independent schools and is not usually helpful to marketing efforts."

— Paul F. Cruikshank, Jr.
Board Chair, Lake Forest Academy

WHAT TO LOOK FOR IN A CONSULTANT

- Articulateness; ability to synthesize ideas
- Knowledge of independent school milieu
- Success with previous independent school clients
- On-time completion of projects

HOW TO FRAME THE RELATIONSHIP

- Faculty, head, and board should all "buy in" to the process.
- Appoint one person as staff liaison.
- Don't pressure the consultant to make specific recommendations.
- Don't wait too long to act on appropriate recommendations; diagnosed situation may change.
- Keep in contact after the assignment is complete; her/his knowledge qualifies her/him to be a valuable sounding board for future issues.

Material drawn from a session at the 1989 NAIS Conference: "Marketing Consultant: Management Resource or Institutional Shrink?" This session was presented by the following members of the Lake Forest Academy, IL, administrative team: Paul Cruikshank, Jr., Board Chair; Tom Hodgkins, President; Mary Ann Hodgkins, Principal; Jacquie Leinbach, Director of Admission. Further ideas were gathered from Independent School Management's "Ideas and Perspectives," October, 1986.

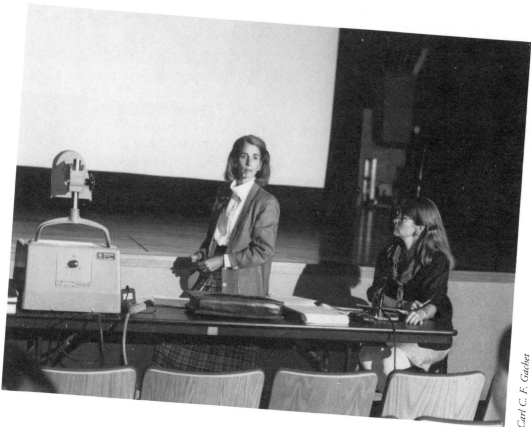

Carl C. F. Gachet

will be confidential. The presence of an outsider may be unsettling for some, while reassuring for others. Know that the initial phases of a consultant's work may seem like another set of tasks to be juggled. Yet the extra time given at the front end of the project will lead to better results.

10) Recognize the long term benefits of a consultant relationship. The consultant's knowledge of your school makes her or him a valuable sounding board for future issues. Never hesitate to ask for an opinion. Some consultancies include ongoing advising as part of the base fee. As a knowledgeable advocate of your school, the consultant can provide valuable insight and guidance.

CHOOSE CAREFULLY, USE WISELY

Remember that the best consultants are partners in problem-solving who can provide fresh ideas and frame appropriate strategies. They will not have all the answers. Nor can they be the sole owners of your project's goals. But if you choose them carefully, use them wisely, and put them shoulder-to-shoulder with your key administrators, you and your school will achieve many more of your marketing goals than you could have alone.

Whitney Ransome's wide experience of independent education includes service as a teacher, dean, admission and financial aid officer and trustee. Currently she is a principal consultant for Marketing and Enrollment Associates, a firm specializing in marketing and communications for independent schools and their associations. In addition to serving as a consultant to over seventy-five independent schools, she has worked at the Ransom-Everglades School (FL), Dana Hall School (MA), and Concord Academy (MA). Whitney is a trustee of the Asheville School (NC), The Willow Hill School (MA), and the Nashoba Brooks School (MA) and an executive director of the Coalition of Girls' Schools.

CHAPTER 16: IN SEARCH OF DIVERSITY
Multicultural Marketing

HEATHER HOERLE

BEYOND GOOD INTENTIONS

Bryn Mawr College's Director of Institutional Diversity reminds educators that institutions cannot overcome serious obstacles to racial equity through passive benevolence. Regularly, Joyce Miller queries, "How can you become as effective for equality as you are well meaning toward it?" The answer, as chronicled in advice below, is to formulate an action plan that will change your institution and the people in it. To make your plan work, it takes more than committed leadership. It takes, in Miller's words, "a sense of urgency."

The United States and its citizens will continue to diversify in the coming decade. African Americans, Hispanic and Latino Americans, Asian Americans, American Indians and Pacific Islanders together will constitute the majority of our nation by 2030. Indeed, as we struggle to be more inclusive and pluralistic in our schools, self-professed good intentions are not enough to advance a multicultural agenda. Demographic realities demand that independent schools work towards heterogeneity or risk becoming obsolete.

MODELS FOR ACTION AND ACCOUNTABILITY

Luckily, there are models of strong multicultural programs readily available for replication by independent schools. In recent years a number of colleges, universities and graduate schools have been proactive in determining and supporting pluralistic communities. Many national and international corporations no longer just suggest, but *expect* that their employees commit to a multicultural environment. XEROX Chairman David Kearns feels that diversity must be " a corporate value, a management priority, and a formal business objective in the 1990's." Assuming that attitudes change from the daily experience of a diverse workplace, XEROX has set a strategy to increase numbers of

Gaining perspective

What does it feel like for a family of color to apply to your school?

This exercise is designed to help refine your school's message to families of color. Try it with your admission/marketing staff:

STUDENT PROFILE

Terri Patterson is a 14-year-old African American enrolled in the 9th grade at Fort Hunt High School. She has grown up in the local area, excelled at soccer, been active on the debate team, and scored well on national tests. Though a successful student, Terri is academically undisciplined. She is adept at finishing her homework quickly, and often takes "the easy way out" with assignments. Socially, Terri is popular and she is part of the "in crowd" in her school. Her parents believe Terri could achieve more in a new school setting and are considering private school to help challenge their daughter in new ways.

INSTRUCTIONS

You are Terri's parent considering an independent school for the first time. You have been sent a school video, viewbook/catalog package and a letter that encourages you to visit the campus.

1) Break into small groups and read the above profile carefully. (Other student bios are available from NAIS Department of Diversity.)

2) Review your school video/slide show and publications.

• How many students of color do you see represented in leadership positions, on athletic fields, in the arts?

• How many teachers of color can you identify in the school's publications?

3) Do your best to answer these questions:

• As parents of color, having reviewed this tape and viewbook, would you send your child to a private school? Why or why not?

• What messages and images worked? Why?

• What messages and images alienated or troubled you?

people of color in each division and at each level by 1995. In creating quantifiable goals, XEROX is holding itself accountable to investors and its board alike.

PUTTING YOUR SCHOOL ON THE MAP

NAIS Director of Diversity Randolph Carter laughs when asked about setting quantifiable goals. "People of color don't mind goal setting, so long as it's not just lip service! Achievable, definable goals are the only real way that institutions can set and measure their progress towards equity." Carter's department offers member schools a number of important services to help with creating genuine multicultural communities. People of Color regional job fairs, an annual diversity workshop, multicultural resource lists, and the Multicultural Assessment Project (MAP), an institutional audit, are services provided to all NAIS member schools. Paula Elliott, MAP's Director, underscores the importance of undergoing a school self study before conducting outreach to families of color. "A number of schools are still in the 'heroes and holidays' mentality and have not fully integrated a multicultural program. The MAP offers every school an opportunity to go beyond the quick fix and to look at the long-term benefits of a pluralistic educational environment."

The NAIS Department of Diversity has learned valuable marketing lessons as a result of their ongoing work with member schools. Listed below are suggestions for building a marketing program that will sustain your current school community, and encourage more participation from new families of color.

• Though demographic predictions are pushing for institutional change, don't let that be your only reason for change.

• Expect multiculturalism to be an ongoing process.

• Review your school's mission statement, making sure it is pluralistic in tone and content.

• Realize that schools must set achievable goals in order to quantify success.

• In creating goals, use national norms as your guide.

• Conduct an institutional audit (e.g., MAP) and involve every community member— students, teachers, maintenance employees, alumni. Do this before you begin marketing to families of color.

• Create forums at your school for discussion of racism, sexism, and classism.

Bringing diversity to your school

Tips from veteran multicultural marketers

Recently, Boarding Schools convened a group of diversity experts to share particular programs. All agreed on one essential feature in their outreach to families of color—Action! An admission officer from a large boarding school in the Northeast explained, "For years, my school talked about the desire for a more diverse community. Still the admission office had to play a leadership role in moving the school towards that goal. We worked internally to make the school more aware, did a better job orienting students of color, and then began work in local communities with people of color." Similar wisdom is reflected in the marketing suggestions below.

From Drew Casertano, Head, Millbrook School, NY

- Work regionally with local churches and ethnic specific organizations to cultivate an understanding of boarding schools.

- Get involved with local African American, Latino, Asian American, and Native American communities sponsoring cooperative events.

- Use school publications to support your commitment to diversity.

From Judy Beams, Director of Admission, Cushing Academy, MA

- Educate yourself about different cultures by getting off campus! Set up meetings with key officials in ethnic specific organizations that you would like to know better.

- Identify several teachers/counselors at your school who will act as special advisors and advocates for students of color.

- Listen to parents of color and their needs. Alter your program in ways that will lessen their fears.

From Will Graham, Director of Admission, Gould Academy, ME

- Offer easy access to information about your school. Without an independent school heritage, many students of color feel alienated from the admission process.

- Tailor your communication to the needs of a specific group... Asian Americans have different questions about boarding school than Native Americans.

From Neville Lake, Associate Director of Admission, Milton Academy, MA

- Design an orientation program specifically for students of color and involve their parents. Introduce the students to the daily regimen of boarding school by setting up "mock" classes, sports events, and study halls.

- Validate the fears of students of color... don't dismiss them!

- Have a strong peer support network for students of color at your school.

From Karen Suplee Hallowell, Director of Admission, George School, PA

- Celebrate diversity in your school—in the dining hall, on the bulletin boards, in assembly programs, in your classrooms.

- Hold people in the community accountable to pluralism. Make diversity central to the school mission through board mandates.

- Convene a task force of current parents, alumni and students of color and identify areas in need of improvement. Be willing to hear criticism. Utilize the talents of this group in changing your school and in attracting new students of color.

- Get to know other educators in ethnic-specific neighborhoods near your school.

- Set quantifiable goals for having more students and faculty of color in your school by the year 2000. Check your progress every 2 years.

- Identify and question traditions in your community that are exclusive and promote homogeneity (e.g., hazing, all-white alumni pictures).
- Ask your alums, parents and students of color for help in making your school more supportive of diversity.
- Understand that solid education and democratic education is multicultural, gender-fair education.

Demographic realities demand that independent schools work towards heterogeneity or risk becoming obsolete.

"JUST DO IT."

There is no paucity of resources available to schools with an interest in multicultural marketing. A Better Chance, The Albert G. Oliver Program, ASPIRA, the NAACP, Jack and Jill of America, the American Indian Science and Engineering Society — these organizations, to name a few, have served as educational advocates to students of color for years. Nearly 50 NAIS member schools have undergone the Multicultural Assessment Project and are willing to work in partnership with your school to build more tolerant and inclusive communities. Many of these schools have noted increased enrollments over the last few years, and attribute some of their success directly to the MAP experience. George School Admission Director Karen Hallowell believes her recruitment and retention success is linked to a positive institutional culture partly generated by the MAP.

Actions do speak louder than words for those who wish to advance a multicultural agenda at an independent school. Rhetoric will not move your school from "status quo" to reform. A recent issue of Deerfield Academy's alumni magazine summarized the best advice for a school interested in multicultural marketing. The cover reads, "Just do it."

KEY QUESTIONS
- What images do visiting families of color have of your school?
- How is a multicultural agenda promoted on your campus?
- What are your current numbers of students and staff of color? What should they be to mirror the percentages in the United States' population in the next 10 years?
- How has your school handled the concerns of families and students of color in the past? How might they be handled differently in the future?
- Has your school successfully retained a large percentage of students of color? Why or why not?

DIVERSITY MARKETING RESOURCES

A Better Chance, 419 Boylston Street, Boston, MA 02116, 617/421-0950
contact: Barbara Booth
A Better Chance (ABC) identifies, recruits and places academically talented and motivated students of color into leading independent secondary schools and selected public school programs.

The Albert G. Oliver Program, 420 Lexington Avenue, Suite 1830, New York, NY 10170, 212/972-3820
contact: John Hoffman
The Albert G. Oliver program places 50 Black and Hispanic students in leading independent schools every year. The program offers community service and guaranteed summer jobs to its students.

AISES (American Indian Science and Engineering Society), 1085 14th Street, Suite 1506, Boulder, CO 80302, 303/492-8658
contact: Norbert Hill
AISES seeks to motivate and encourage American Indian students in the fields of science, engineering and technology. The organization offers scholarships for college-level work, holds teacher training workshops, and has student chapters in colleges and universities.

ASPIRA of America, Inc., 1112 16th Street, NW, Suite 340, Washington, DC 20036, 202/835-3600
contact: Dr. Juan Rosario
ASPIRA is a community-based leadership development organization working to increase access for Puerto Ricans and other Hispanics to quality educational opportunities.

The Next Marketing Handbook for Independent Schools

Jack and Jill of America,
    1065 Gordon Street, SW, Atlanta, GA 30310,
    404/753-8471
    contact: Patricia Cannon
    Jack and Jill of America is an organization for
    parents of color interested in "PEP"—parenting,
    education and political involvement. JJA has 7
    regional groups and 180 local groups.

**NAACP (National Association for the Advance-
    ment of Colored People),**
    4805 Mt. Hope Drive, Baltimore, MD 21215,
    301/358-8900
    contact: Dr. Beverly Cole
    The NAACP offers scholarships for undergradu-
    ate/graduate students who are attending college
    or university in the US full-time. With many
    regional chapters, independent schools are
    encouraged to actively pursue collaborative
    work in their local areas.

**NAIS Department of Diversity and
    Multicultural Services,**
    75 Federal Street, Boston, MA 02110,
    617/451-2444
    contact: Randolph Carter
    The NAIS Department of Diversity and
    Multicultural Services offers assistance to
    member schools in developing strategies to
    improve diversity of their student bodies;
    multicultural curricular resources; a job bank for
    people of color; training in the areas of diversity,
    antiracism, and issues of class; and the
    Multicultural Assessment Plan, an evaluative
    instrument to review the current status of school
    diversity efforts.

*Heather Hoerle has been an independent school aficio-
nado ever since she got over her sophomore homesick-
ness as a boarder at Westtown School (PA). She is currently associate director of Boarding Schools, a marketing consortium representing over 240 boarding schools
in North America and Europe. Heather began her career as a teacher, dorm parent, administrator, and
stage director at The George School (PA) and The
Westtown School. Prior to joining the Boarding
Schools' staff in 1988, she earned an M.A. at The
Harvard Graduate School of Education. In 1989
Heather developed the Boarding Schools Diversity
Marketing Network, an initiative designed to help
member schools attract and retain students of color.*

The Multicultural Assessment Plan (MAP)—
A Service of the National Association of Independent Schools

The MAP is designed to build schoolwide responsibility for multicultural
principles and practices that translate into excellent education for all students. Schools that elect to undergo the MAP conduct a guided self study
that includes administration, government, faculty, curriculum, climate,
support services, development and public relations. The MAP structure is
similar to the regional evaluation process to which schools are accustomed. The actual self assessment process typically takes approximately 5–
7 months with the completed report sent to NAIS MAP staff for review.
This is followed by an evaluation team visit to the school. The Department of Diversity and Multicultural Services and MAP staff become allies
and resources to the school as it works to become a more authentic and
equitable multicultural educational community.

CHAPTER 17: ALLIES IN THE CLASSROOM
Teachers and Marketing

STEVE CLEM

Marketing today is not a function; it is a way of doing business. Marketing is not a new ad campaign or this month's promotion. Marketing has to be all-pervasive, part of everyone's job description, from the receptionists to the board of directors. Its job is neither to fool the customer nor to falsify the company's image. It is to integrate the customer into the design of the product and to design a systematic process for interaction that will create substance in the relationship.

—Regis McKenna, *Marketing is Everything*

LIBERATING THE ADMISSION OFFICER WITHIN EACH TEACHER

You do not have to stretch too hard to transfer McKenna's thoughts about marketing in the corporate world to the world of independent education. Consider the fundamental message and the vocabulary: eschewing the old "snake oil" associations with marketing, McKenna stresses honesty, integration, interaction and the creation of substantive, ongoing relationships with customers. Don't we want all of those things in our schools? And his first point is perhaps the most important: marketing is part of everyone's job description. Teachers are, I believe, your best potential marketers, but they also may be the most resistant to this seemingly new—but not really new—facet of their job. Where does that resistance come from? What can you do to help faculty see their work in this new light? What can faculty themselves do to most effectively promote the school, its people and its programs? This chapter addresses these questions.

For the first six or seven years of my career as a full-time teacher in independent schools, admission was like electricity for me: taken for granted and poorly understood. And while I came gradually to understand what the admission folks did, I certainly never saw myself as being a part of the process. When times were especially good, and demand always exceeded supply, it was easy, as a teacher, to stay distant from what appeared to be a fairly perfunctory business. We had, it seems to me now, a kind of superior attitude toward virtually everyone in the school who wasn't a teacher, the classic response to being at the bottom of the totem pole, in terms of real power and salary. We didn't have much, but we had our superiority.

We accepted the good students that came to the school as being, somehow, our due and it never occurred to us to thank the admission officer for his or her part in getting the student to come. On the other hand, when there was a problem with a new student, we found our way quickly to the admission office to decry (pick one or more) lowering standards, favoritism, or temporary lapses of judgment.

Even when times turned bad and enrollment was dropping, it still didn't occur to me that there might be a very real connection between the kind of job we were doing in the classroom and the number and quality of students applying to the school. It took two years of salary freezes and cuts in staff at my school for me to understand that admission and marketing were part of my job too, and that I couldn't stand off to the side like some detached Greek chorus, commenting on what was happening and pretending I wasn't involved.

Clearly not everyone is as thick as I was, but I suspect I was not atypical and the very existence of this chapter suggests that there is some kind of attitudinal gap that needs to be bridged. William Sloane Coffin once said that the woman that most needed liberation was the woman inside each man. Maybe it's time to think about liberating the admission officer in every teacher and the teacher in every admission officer.

WHY SHOULD TEACHERS CARE ABOUT MARKETING?

Assuming the gap between the admission office and the classroom can be bridged, why is it worth doing?

- Mutual understanding and support among internal constituencies are crucial to the school's mission.

- Many admissions people, like many faculty, sometimes feel isolated and misunderstood; loneliness may be endemic to schools, but you can work against it, thereby enhancing both effectiveness and job satisfaction.

- Every single contact with a prospective or current or former student or parent is a marketing opportunity; people need to know how to make the most of those opportunities.

Of course, like Molière's Monsieur Jourdain who was so delighted to learn that he'd been speaking prose all his life, teachers and everyone else in the school have always been marketing the school, for better or for worse. The point is to make good marketing a conscious exercise so that the messages you send are, indeed, the messages you want to send. Teachers are crucial allies in this process.

Maybe it's time to think about liberating the admission officer in every teacher and the teacher in every admission officer.

Steve Clem is the director of academic services at NAIS. Over the course of his eighteen-year career in independent schools Steve was a French teacher, a department head and an upper school head. As part of NAIS's Promoting Independent Education Project, Steve has had the opportunity to learn a great deal about marketing in general, and the marketing of schools in particular. That new knowledge helped Steve see his time in schools in a different light and led to this chapter on the role of teachers in promoting schools.

Contexts for cooperation

Here are some concrete steps that admission officers and teachers can take to help each other and their schools.

WHAT CAN ADMISSION OFFICERS DO TO ENLIST TEACHER SUPPORT FOR MARKETING?

◆ Acquire a wide repertoire of stories that describe the quality of the teaching in the school and that highlight particular faculty successes in meeting the needs of individual students.

◆ Use rich narratives of good teaching in your admissions material.

◆ Visit departmental, divisional or grade-level meetings to hear what's on people's minds.

◆ Get teachers on the admissions committee and use them well.

◆ Provide specific training or suggestions to faculty whose classes will be visited by prospective students or parents. Ask them for brief descriptions of what will be happening in the class so that visitors have some sense of context.

◆ Try to avoid unscheduled visits. The very presence of a visitor can "throw" a teacher, veteran or rookie. If you can't avoid some "drop-ins," be sure you know which teachers can accommodate them most easily. Remind faculty that affective impressions (correct or not) will play a major role in the family's decision.

◆ Shadow a student for a day at various grade levels. What does it really feel like to be student in your school?

◆ Ask teachers to suggest possible students from neighborhoods, church contacts, or local athletic leagues for kids. Give them special cards to attach a note to admission material.

◆ Communicate with curriculum leaders to ensure that you can articulate, at least in broad strokes, the school's program.

◆ Give the faculty regular feedback on what you are hearing from prospective students and parents.

◆ If the admissions portfolio includes writing samples or samples of other kinds of student work, ask faculty to help you judge the strengths of the pieces submitted. And consider having teachers contact strong candidates with some response to the pieces; many small colleges are using this approach.

◆ Once new students are enrolled, enlist faculty help in keeping attrition to a minimum. What does the new student need and how can you sustain these efforts beyond the orientation process?

◆ Review your admission material. Is the faculty actually doing what your literature says they do? If not, bring it up.

◆ As you conduct market research, look for ways to involve interested faculty.

◆ Enlist faculty help in editing/designing publications and in producing videos, or critiquing the work of your designer or producer. Use their talents as much as you can.

◆ When controversy is in the air in school, be sure faculty have the best possible information and language to use to explain situations to people outside the school. What will they say when, for example, the visiting parent or student asks about a recent disciplinary situation? How will they respond, when cornered in the local supermarket, to questions about the Board's latest decision about X?

◆ Use admission case studies with faculty groups to get at important issues and promote a greater understanding of the complexities of admission decisions.

◆ Have faculty offer short workshops for prospective students and parents, or workshops on, say, study skills, for anyone in the community.

◆ Give the faculty a brief talk on demographics, financial aid, and testing.

◆ If you make a mistake, say so, and expect others to do the same.

- Involve faculty in defining academic transition strategies for new students.
- Be sure to let the head and division heads know which faculty have been particularly helpful.
- Seek ways that the school can reward faculty who contribute meaningfully to the process. People pay attention to which behaviors get reinforced.
- Publicize teacher and student accomplishments in the local media.
- Support school programs for faculty development; the eventual payoff is better teaching and a better school to promote. Be an advocate for better faculty compensation and anything that promotes the professionalization of teachers.
- Beware of pre-cooked lists (like this one) and get faculty to help you create your own.

WHAT CAN TEACHERS DO TO BE BETTER MARKETERS?

- We need to understand and accept our collective and individual responsibility for the school's reputation. This is scary and a powerful topic for in-depth conversation at a faculty retreat. What is our reputation? Is that what we want? How can we change it? or be sure to sustain it? What can I do in my classroom to change how the school is perceived?
- Every faculty member should be able to explain the basics of the school's admissions process to anyone who might ask. What is the process? What are the criteria? When should one apply? How do you apply for financial aid?
- Each teacher in the school should ask himself or herself the following question on a regular basis: "How can I demonstrate by my actions and my words that our school is worth it?" This may be uncomfortable at first, but everyone must understand that this is the question hard-pressed parents ask.
- Teachers should keep admissions and public relations staff aware of special programs and successes and of potential problems.
- You need to remember that prospective students are far more interested in the affect of a class than the content. The visiting student is asking himself or herself: Is there a place for me here? Will I fit in? Can I do the work? Will I be safe? Will I stick out somehow? How will the teachers treat me?
- If a prospective student has visited your class,

you could send a brief note thanking them for coming, and offer to answer any questions the student or parents might have about your class, division or department.

- In a multiple-division school, with clear transition points, faculty *on both sides of the transition* need to transcend intramural disagreements and stress the value of the division just left and the division to be entered. Don't try to make yourself look good at the expense of some other part of the school.

- Your present students and parents are your most important promoters; keep reminding them of how smart their investment was and give them the language to talk about what you do to others.
- Seek and use feedback from your students. The very act of asking makes them feel better about you and the school.
- Airing internal conflicts with parents or students may be satisfying in the short term but it hurts the school in the long run. And what hurts the school hurts you.
- Everything that goes home—every single piece of paper—reflects on the school and is a marketing occasion, whether you want it to be or not. We should practice looking over what we send home from the perspective of both the current parent and a prospective parent.
- Teachers, more than anyone else, have the opportunity for frequent and fruitful contacts with parents, directly or indirectly. While those contacts are centered on the child's progress, they are laden with messages, explicit and implicit, about the school. Think about the messages you send via your phone calls, written comments, formal conferences and informal conversations.
- Parents are constantly making judgments about the school based on what they hear around the dinner table or during vacations. Each teacher should try answering the following question on a regular basis: "What do I hope my students say about me and my teaching?"
- Teachers can write articles on education issues for school publications, but also for local newspapers. You can seek occasions in the larger community to speak out on issues important to it. This reflects favorably on the school.

Understanding the International Market

MARY PETERSON

Few will disagree that the world is shrinking. Educators and administrators in the independent school sector have the opportunity to infuse our students' education with effective, face to face intercultural awareness. We have the opportunity to reduce the tensions rooted in persons having only distant, stereotypical impressions of the differences which distinguish races and nationalities. Personalizing these differences allows us to be more understanding and tolerant and to minimize the divisiveness of prejudice.

Few will argue, as well, with the premise that students from around the world enrich our classrooms and campus life experiences. The meticulous accuracy and artistic sensitivity of Japanese musicians, the challenge for American youth to keep pace with the strong science and math talents of their Korean classmates, the wonderful free spirit of European students, and the academic acumen and incredibly warm personalities of Thai students all enrich our increasingly diverse school communities and help us grow in our respect for people from other countries and cultures.[1]

Independent schools have the capability to educate the world's future leaders. And, in so doing, they have the opportunity to enrich the learning they provide to all their students. International students can bring the world to the school, enabling the faculty to teach not just about the world, but from it.

WHAT'S ALL THIS FUSS ABOUT "INTERNATIONALIZATION"?

International students are one component of an international education, i.e., an education that prepares the way for today's youth to live in tomorrow's world. There are many who would say that every child deserves access to this type of education,

---

1. *The International Imperative: Report of the International Task Force*, Boarding Schools, Secondary School Admission Test Board and NAFSA: Association of International Educators, October 1991, page 3.

but there are few schools that have developed coordinated programs to provide it.

Besides having a diverse population of international students and utilizing them as educational resources, there are several other components schools can consider developing if an international dimension is consistent with their missions. These include, among others:

- ◆ opportunities for American students to study abroad
- ◆ opportunities for faculty to travel, do research, or take sabbaticals abroad
- ◆ sister school relationships
- ◆ international studies
- ◆ foreign languages
- ◆ infusing the curriculum with an international perspective
- ◆ intercultural programs on campus

As no two schools are identical, no two will choose the same balance of components in realizing the international dimensions of their missions. Too often, however, schools drift or dive into international recruitment without considering the risks involved and the impact that their success (or failure) will have on the school. In these cases, school personnel can expend vast amounts of energy in keeping the international programs as close to problem-free as possible, and never see the positive side of the balance sheet—educationally, culturally, or economically—at all.

Whatever decisions are made about international education, they will affect the entire school. For purposes of planning, as well as estimating impact of changes in the foreign student population, an exercise is provided on page 110. Once the policy issues have been clarified, operational decisions become much simpler, and the principles and techniques of marketing outlined in the rest of this book can be meaningfully adapted to the international context.

Achieving international diversity, i.e., having students from many foreign countries on campus, may be more difficult than admitting a large group from one or two countries but it is a goal well worth striving for. Educationally and culturally, the learning environment is more likely to sparkle. In terms of campus life, the international students will be less likely to huddle in their own groups. And economically, admitting students from several countries puts the school much less at risk of waking up one morning to find out that unanticipated world events have precipitated a serious cash flow crisis for the students and the school.

On that note, a word about ethics is in order. In the late 1970s, international student recruitment practice by some institutions earned a bad name for the activity and did serious damage to the reputation of U.S. education in some countries. Since that time, a support system has been put in place to assist international student recruiters. NAFSA: Association of International Educators, the professional organization for persons and institutions concerned with educational exchange, operates a clearinghouse

---

International students can bring the world to the school, enabling the faculty to teach not just about the world, but from it.

---

that monitors the activities of third-party recruiters and can provide information on placement agencies operating abroad. NAFSA makes available its code of ethics, helps with foreign credential evaluation and provides workshops, consultants' services, conferences and publications that can assist schools in evaluating and strengthening their international programs and their international recruitment efforts.

WHAT DOES THE INTERNATIONAL MARKET LOOK LIKE?

Because data on foreign students at the elementary and secondary levels are so hard to come by, it is helpful to examine flows and trends at the postsecondary level. Except as noted below, all figures used in this section are based on data provided by the Institute of International Education in *Open Doors 1989-90* and *Profiles 1987-88*.

Foreign Students Around the World. According to UNESCO, just over one million students are currently studying outside their home countries. About one-third of them (407,529 in 1990-91) are enrolled in United States colleges and universities. Other nations that receive the largest numbers of foreign students are France (126,762 in 1986), Germany (81,724 in 1986), the Soviet Union (62,942 in 1986), United Kingdom (56,726 in 1986), Italy (29,447 in 1986), Canada (27,210 in 1986) and Japan (14,960 in 1986, estimated at 40,000 presently).

Although foreign student numbers in the United States have climbed steadily over the past 40 years, the rate of growth has fluctuated widely. These patterns are illustrated in Figure 1.

Figure 1
Foreign Students in the U.S. [1954/55 – 1989/90]

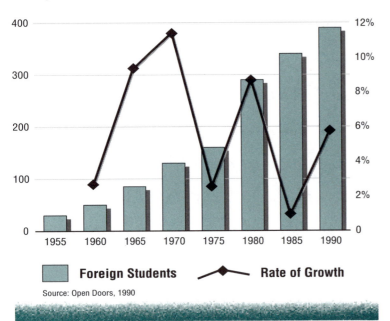

Foreign Students ◆ **Rate of Growth**

Source: Open Doors, 1990

Unlike the United States, most other major host nations have centralized mechanisms for setting policy on educational exchange, and several have policies that actively encourage recruitment of overseas students. Japan, for example, aspires to have 100,000 foreign students by the year 2000. The United Kingdom, through the British Council, operates overseas offices that recruit students and sponsor educational fairs. Britain also offers a significant program of scholarships for students from Commonwealth countries. Australia, whose policy has been variable over the past decade, now sponsors overseas offices that offer "one-stop shopping" for prospective students in a free market recruitment environment.

Like the U.S., however, other major host countries are experiencing very low or actually negative rates of population growth. Virtually all of them will be seeking to increase their foreign student populations during the 1990s, and it is a fair prediction that competition among host nations will increase. It is also worth noting that some countries, e.g., Japan and the Newly Industrialized Countries of East Asia, which are both senders and receivers of international students, will be experiencing shifts on both sides of the educational exchange equation. The impacts of new regional relationships in Europe, Asia and the Western hemisphere remain to be seen.

Foreign Students in the United States. Among the major host countries, the U.S. is least saturated with foreign students, with 2.8% of its total postsecondary student population in the category of nonimmigrant foreigners. Of foreign students in the U.S., 44% are graduate students, 35.5% are seeking a bachelor's degree, 12% are in associate degree programs, and 4.4% are enrolled in intensive English language programs.

Roughly three-quarters of the financial support for foreign students in the U.S. comes from foreign sources. About two-thirds of all foreign students are supported with personal and family funds. U.S. colleges and universities support 18% (largely at the graduate level), the U.S. government sponsors just over 2%, and U.S. private sponsors support another 3%. The remainder comes from home governments, foreign private sponsors, employers and international organizations.

Students report that their decisions to go overseas for education are made predominantly on the basis of educational opportunity in a particular field. In making their decisions, they report being most influenced by family, friends and teachers. Other factors that correlate with out-migrations of students include political and religious developments (especially in times of upheaval in the home country), economic developments (presence of a wealthy upper and perhaps upper-middle class, surges in national revenues, currency fluctuations), and educational development (inability of the home education system to accommodate sufficient number of students at a particular level). Among developed nations, students more often consider personal experience an important factor.

Who Chooses the United States? Patterns of students' choice of a foreign country in which to study are linked to several factors, including long-standing historical (colonial) relationships, political and economic ties, geographic proximity, and relative currency strengths. While Africans tend to go to France (42%, vs. 16% to the U.S.), and Europeans show a slight tendency to go to Germany (18.4%, vs. 18.1% to the U.S.), students from other regions tend to choose the United States (58.5% of Asians, 32.5% of Latin Americans, 23% of Middle Eastern students, 37% of North Americans, and 47.2% of Oceanian students).

At the postsecondary level, countries sending the most students to the United States are illustrated in Table 1. For purposes of independent school marketing, a list of the countries with the

The Next Marketing Handbook for Independent Schools

Table 1 COUNTRIES WITH THE MOST FOREIGN STUDENTS IN U.S. COLLEGES AND UNIVERSITIES, 1990-91

China	39,600	Canada	18,350
Japan	38,610	Malaysia	13,610
Taiwan	33,530	Hong Kong	12,630
India	28,860	Indonesia	9,520
S. Korea	23,360	Pakistan	7,730

largest numbers of students seeking bachelor's degrees and the highest proportions of students enrolled in private educational institutions is provided in Table 2. (Note: Total numbers of students are not provided for these countries, as *Profiles* data from which the calculations were made are based on a sample, rather than a census of students.)

Table 2 COUNTRIES WITH THE MOST FOREIGN STUDENTS SEEKING BACHELOR'S DEGREES AND ATTENDING U.S. PRIVATE COLLEGES

Canada	Nigeria	Thailand
Malasia	India	China
Japan	Indonesia	Germany
Hong Kong	Taiwan	Philippines
Korea	Pakistan	Venezuela
United Kingdom	Iran	Mexico

DISTRIBUTION OF FOREIGN STUDENTS WITHIN INDEPENDENT SCHOOLS

NAIS annually collects and publishes data on international students attending active member institutions within the continental United States. These data reveal that the total student population in independent schools was 2.4% international in 1989-90, and that that percentage has grown annually over a three year period. While the numbers of international students in day-boarding and day schools remained relatively stable in the two most recent years, the numbers in boarding schools jumped by almost 50% between 1988-89 and 1989-90. Boarding schools are now upwards of 10% international students, compared to 1.1% in day schools.

As shown in figure 3, the highest current proportions of international students are found in boarding, secondary and single-sex schools. And, while the raw numbers of international students may not be as high in those types of schools, the percent of total student body is a critical factor to consider as recruitment plans are made.

Regionally, international students are diffused across the nation's independent schools, with 28% attending schools in the Northeast, compared to 11%–15% in each other region. Independent school populations in the Northeast are 4% international, compared to 3% for the Southwest region, 2.5% for Western schools, 2.2% in the Midwest, and 1.8% in each of the other three regions. As noted above, data

Figure 2
Growth in Numbers of Foreign Students in Independent Schools

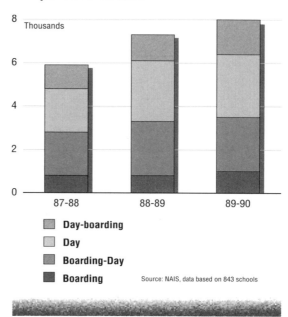

Source: NAIS, data based on 843 schools

Figure 3
Foreign Students in Independent Schools
By Type of School, 1989/90

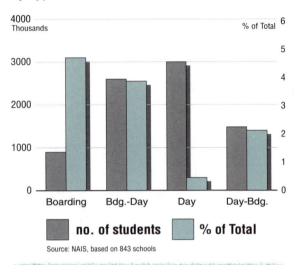

Source: NAIS, based on 843 schools

Figure 4
Where Foreign Students Go in the U.S.
Independent Schools, 1989/90

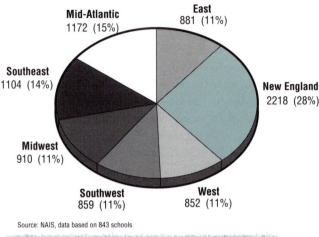

Source: NAIS, data based on 843 schools

in this section are based on an NAIS survey, to which 843 active member institutions responded.

Tendencies of students from particular world regions and countries to attend schools in particular locations in the U.S. will be discussed below.

CHARACTERISTICS OF STUDENTS AND RECRUITMENT OUTLOOK BY WORLD REGION

This section draws upon information prepared by June Noronha of the College of St. Catherine, as well as the statistical reference books published by IIE.

AFRICA. Ten years ago, Africans made up 13% of the foreign student population in the United States; today they represent only 8% of the total. Major African sending countries are Nigeria, South Africa, Egypt, Kenya and Ethiopia. More than half the postsecondary African students come as undergraduates. Among foreign students, more Africans come to study business/management, education, agriculture, physical sciences and health sciences at the undergraduate level, and fewer come to study engineering, fine arts or math/computer science than do other foreign students. Students from francophone countries generally require English as a Second Language (ESL) instruction, while those from anglophone countries will not. African students exhibit a moderate preference for private institutions in the U.S. (29%, as compared to 20% of U.S. students). Within the U.S., African students tend to enroll in schools in the South, Midwest and

Northeast. Most African students come with personal and family funds, but the availability of financial aid will be extremely important to them. Africa sends a relatively high proportion of males (68.4%), even at the undergraduate level.

At this time, the recruitment outlook for Africa is poor, with the exception of capital cities. In general, Africans exhibit a preference for boarding schools in the United Kingdom and France and many families remain unaware of American independent schools.

ASIA. By far the fastest growing region, Asian students now make up half the postsecondary foreign student population. The top five Asian sending countries are the top five countries worldwide: China, Taiwan, Japan, India and Korea. Of these, China and Taiwan are sending predominantly (approximately 80%) graduate students. Compared to other foreign undergraduate students, more Asians come to study business/management, engineering, math/computer science and fine arts, while fewer are interested in health sciences, education or social sciences. Students from China, Japan, Taiwan, Korea, Thailand and Indonesia generally need ESL instruction, while others are not as likely to require it. About one-third of Asian students enroll in private institutions in the U.S. Almost exactly two-thirds of them are males. They come primarily on personal and family funds, with some government support. Financial aid is important, especially for Chinese students. Within the U.S., Asian students tend to cluster in the Northeast, Pacific and Midwest regions.

The Next Marketing Handbook for Independent Schools

The recruitment outlook for Asia is very good at this time. Government policies affecting younger students in several countries have become more permissive. Many Asian capital cities with strong economies also have large populations of third country nationals. Traditionally, however, Asians have preferred Asian and European boarding schools.

EUROPE. Europeans make up 11% of the foreign student population in the United States. Until data are available for 1991-92, there is little information available on Eastern European student flows, except to say that Yugoslavia and Poland both topped 1,000 students in 1989-90. Students from Western Europe have traditionally accounted for about 96% of students from the region, with the United Kingdom, Germany, France, Greece and Spain in the lead. Half of the postsecondary students from Europe come as undergraduates, and about 60% of those are men. Compared to other foreign students, European undergraduates are more likely to study fine arts, humanities, education, physical sciences and social sciences, and less likely to enroll for engineering, math/computer science or health sciences. Relatively few Europeans will require ESL. Supported by personal and family funds, along with some government funding, Western Europeans are less likely to need financial aid than other foriegn student groups. Within the U.S., Europeans are found mostly in the Northeast, South and Midwest and have the highest percentage (45%) enrolled in private institutions of any regional group of foreign students.

Although their numbers have not kept pace with other regions over the last 20 years, Europe is worth watching. Historically, Europeans have preferred boarding schools within the region. It remains to be seen whether the breaking down of national educational and trade boundaries in 1992 will mean that fewer students—or more students—will go outside Europe to study. In addition, there are growing numbers of third country nationals in many European cities.

LATIN AMERICA. With 48,090 students in 1989-90, Latin Americans make up 12.4% of the postsecondary population of foreign students. Over the years, this region has accounted for a smaller and smaller share of the population. Student numbers, which had declined since the debt crisis of the early 1980s, have now begun to recover. Major sending nations are Mexico, Brazil, Colombia, Jamaica and Peru. Latin America sends the highest proportion of undergraduates (68.7%) and the highest proportion of female undergraduates

(43.7%). Compared to other foreign students, Latin American undergraduates are more likely to study agriculture, education, fine arts, health sciences, social sciences and other fields, and less likely to enroll in business/management (except for Mexicans and Peruvians), engineering (except for Venezuelans), or math/computer science (except for Mexicans and Venezuelans). In general, Latin Americans require ESL instruction. Financial aid is very important to this group, supported largely by personal and family funds. Within the U.S., a large percentage of Latin Americans are concentrated in schools in the South and Southwest.

The recruitment outlook for Latin America is improving, but will depend largely on the economic picture. Latin Americans are more aware of the existence of American boarding schools than are other regions, and are traditionally split between U.S. and European boarding schools. Capital cities hold some promise, particularly where the economy is strong enough to maintain groups of third country nationals.

MIDDLE EAST. In 1979-80, there were 83,700 Middle Eastern students in U.S. colleges and universities, accounting for nearly 30% of the foreign student population. In 1989-90, the numbers have dropped to 37,330, and are less than 10% of the total. Countries with the largest numbers of students are Iran, Jordan, Lebanon, Saudi Arabia and Turkey, although the last three declined substantially in the past year. Kuwait, which had dropped out of the top five, may need to send more students during its period of rebuilding. About 63% of Middle Eastern students are undergraduates, and of those, 83.7% are males. Compared to other foreign undergraduates, Middle Eastern students are more likely to study engineering, math/computer science and physical sciences, and are less likely to enter business/management, fine arts, humanities or social sciences.

International student brochures and application forms are essential if you want to improve the quality and/or quantity of your international student population.

They are somewhat less likely than other groups to need ESL. Financial aid, while still important to this group, is less critical than to some other regions.

Overall, the recruitment outlook for the Middle East is poor at present, except for groups of third country nationals.

A Word About Changeability. If the last decade has taught international recruiters a lesson, it is that current trends cannot be simply extrapolated into the future. The more involved a school becomes with the international market, the more directly unexpected events in world history will have an impact on the school.

Countries that send large numbers of students today may experience debt crises, demographic declines (although these can be anticipated, as in the case of Japan) or political reversals, or may simply reach a stage of educational development that enables them to retain more of their school age population.

For the record, the countries that have registered the highest levels of change in the numbers of their students in the U.S. in the past year are listed in Table 3, above.

OK, I'M READY. WHERE DO I BEGIN?

Following are several possible recruitment activities. A sound international recruitment program will combine several of these components, according to the school's degree of commitment and availability of resources. This section includes much information that has been adapted from materials originally prepared by Linda Heaney of Linden Educational Services.

Watch the world. By monitoring current world events, you will be able to forecast foreign student population trends and target your recruitment efforts. Pay particular attention to the

Table 3 COUNTRIES WITH THE GREATEST DEGREE OF CHANGE BETWEEN 1988-89 AND 1989-90

Japan	24.3%	Nigeria	–27.2%
Spain	19.3%	Saudi Arabia	–17.3%
Jamaica	17.8%	Iran	–16.9%
Peru	16%	Lebanon	–13.3%
China	15%	Malaysia	–12.2%

value of the U.S. dollar vis-à-vis other currencies, U.S. and foreign government scholarship programs, and countries with expanding economies.

Some ways to do this are:

a) Join international education related associations:

NAFSA: Association of International Educators (1875 Connecticut Avenue, NW, Washington, DC 20009-5278; 202-462-4811)

OREGON EPISCOPAL SCHOOL

Jiyoung Huh, a student at Oregon Episcopal School, is from Seoul, Korea.

Federation of American Boarding Schools
(c/o Pelham Associates, 384 Magothy Road, Severna Park, MD 21146)

Institute of International Education
(809 U.N. Plaza, New York, NY 10017)

America-Mideast Education and Training Services (AMIDEAST) (1100 17th Street, NW, Washington, DC 20036)

b) attend NAFSA regional and national conferences

c) subscribe to the *London Times Higher Education Supplement*

d) attend other conferences, forums, symposia on world affairs

Use the current student network. Your students (past and present) are your most effective recruiters; they can build credibility and name recognition for your school. They can help you by:

a) keeping you current on what's happening in their countries

b) giving you names of friends and family members who may be prospective students

c) identifying schools that should receive mailings

d) taking catalogues and photo albums to their own schools when they return

e) preparing a video presentation for an alumni gathering in their home countries

Tap faculty and senior administrators. Faculty and senior administrators are often the strongest supporters of foreign students and international education. They welcome well-qualified students and appreciate the knowledge they bring to the campus. With proper training, they can help you by:

a) visiting educational advising offices when they travel overseas

b) participating in international professional organizations and identifying joint projects and prospective students

c) gaining press coverage for your institution when traveling overseas to international meetings or on speaking tours

d) identifying overseas institutions which should receive regular mailings

Mobilize your alumni. International alumni appreciate helping their institution and they can be good representatives. To create this network, you need to:

a) find and contact your alumni

b) build your alumni organization with students who are preparing to leave the school—a farewell/welcome to the alumni network party works well

c) see that alumni receive a newsletter on a regular basis

d) train your alumni to represent you at recruitment fairs

e) ask them to interview prospective students for you

Organize the office. Your goal should be an office which can respond to international students with clarity, speed and courtesy. Remember that foreign students often take the first acceptance they receive.

a) use international airmail and courier, when necessary

b) train your staff (and computer) to handle foreign names and addresses

c) anticipate students' questions so they can be answered in one mailing

d) keep your reference library up to date

e) develop consistent country-specific admissions guidelines

f) evaluate transfer credits before issuing the I-20

g) develop country-specific letters if you receive many inquiries from one country

h) monitor your enrolled students' performance to check your admission standards

DEVELOP FOREIGN STUDENT-SPECIFIC MATERIALS

International student brochures and application forms are essential if you want to improve the quality and/or quantity of your international student population. A good international student brochure reflects the institution and is accurate, informative and clear. It includes the following:

a) a general statement of philosophy about the institution

b) accreditation information

c) geographic information: location, climate, community

d) academic information: fields of study

e) financial information: expenses for academic year; summer living expenses; financial aid possibilities or lack thereof; employment possibilities

f) English language requirements and availability of ESL courses

g) health insurance requirements

h) application procedures: forms, fees, test requirements, certified transcripts, recommendation

i) visa information

j) services: foreign student services, housing, health services

The following information is helpful but not necessary:

a) general information on U.S. education

b) transfer credit practices

c) extracurricular activities

d) country-by-country admission requirements

PLAN TARGETED MAILINGS

Overseas direct mailings can be an expensive, unproductive and time-consuming activity. A good mailing campaign is well organized and targeted. It recognizes that key schools and counseling centers need a catalogue and poster and a cover letter with a few brochures. Other schools, government agencies and educational organizations need a cover letter and a few brochures. Some countries will require annual mailings; others may need to be updated (especially with catalogues) less frequently. There are companies, such as Skypak, that offer lower overseas airmail services for U.S. institutions.

The following directories will help you to build your mailing list:

a) **Directory of Overseas Educational Advising Centers** ($7.00)
College Board Publications, Box 886
New York, NY 10106

b) **ISS Directory of Overseas Schools** ($25.00)
P.O. Box 5910
Princeton, NJ 08540

c) **ECIS Directory** (approx. $15.00)
18 Lavant Street
Petersfield, Hampshire GU 3EW
England

d) **Overseas American-Sponsored Elementary and Secondary Schools** Assisted by the U.S. Department of State (free)
Office of Overseas Schools (A/OS)
Room 234, SA-6; U.S. Department of State
Washington, DC 20520

e) **Directory of Department of Defense Schools** (free)
U.S. Department of Defense
Office of Dependents Schools
Room 152, Hoffman Building #1
12461 Eisenhower Avenue
Alexandria, VA 22331

CONTACT SPONSORING AGENCIES

There are embassies and agencies in Washington and New York that are responsible for placing foreign students in American educational institutions and that monitor their progress while they are studying. These agencies are interested in knowing about programs, services, costs and admission procedures at your school. The key is the match; i.e., you need to identify agencies that place students in programs like yours.

If you are interested in receiving exchange students, who usually come for a year or less under the auspices of a youth exchange program, you should become familiar with the organizations listed by the *Council on Standards for International Education Travel* (3 Loudoun Street, SE, Leesburg, VA 22075). This organization annually evaluates teenage exchange programs and produces a listing of those that meet its standards.

Publication Don'ts

When preparing foreign student publications, observe the following DON'Ts:
- use long, complex sentences
- pose students for photos
- use maps of a single state
- use line drawings
- use state abbreviations
- show students of one ethnic group
- use time-dated information (replace "June 1, 1990 to August 15, 1990" with "early June to mid-August")
- show photos of classes on the grass, bare arms or feet, Greek letters, people eating, beards, bald heads
- include 800-numbers or offers to accept collect calls
- use American slang or idiomatic expressions

Source: *Study in the USA*

The Next Marketing Handbook for Independent Schools

ADVERTISE IN OVERSEAS PUBLICATIONS

a) Regional publications for prospective students

Study in the USA – editions are available for Northeast Asia, Latin America, Europe, and the Middle East. (Peggy Printz, editor, 119 South Main St. Suite 220, Seattle, WA 98104; 206-622-2075)

b) Regional commercial publications such as *The Economist, The Far Eastern Economic Review*, etc.

c) Country-specific publications: (1) for students, such as the Hong Kong Express News Education Supplement, several Japanese publications, the PMSI International Journal for Europe; or (2) magazines or newspapers.

PRODUCE AUDIO-VISUAL PRESENTATIONS

Students appreciate audio-visual presentations about American institutions because they do not have the opportunity to make campus visits. Overseas students feel "far away" and are anxious to look at geography, physical facilities and students and faculty. They are particularly helpful and reassuring to students who have been accepted.

Most overseas schools, counseling centers and students have video cassette recorders. Because of difficulties in compatibility, schools are well advised to write to the center, asking about VCR format, before sending the presentation. A video library of U.S. institutions is maintained by Linden Educational Services, 5612 Wilson Lane, Bethesda, MD 20814.

TRAVEL OVERSEAS

The benefits of traveling overseas are two-fold: (1) you get to learn about other countries and their educational systems; and (2) students get to learn

about your institution directly from you. Admission officers find they do a more effective job of admitting successful (and better qualified) candidates when they have traveled overseas. Parents are particularly appreciative of having this opportunity to meet with an adult representative of the institution. You will want to visit educational advisory centers, American and international schools, local schools, colleges, universities and government agencies. You will also want to meet with your alumni and explore the possibility of forming an alumni chapter.

THE WORLD AWAITS YOU

While a good many independent schools do recruit internationally, there are only a few that have constructed a well thought through, consistently applied program of international recruitment. The world awaits the schools that decide to do it right.

Mary E. Peterson is senior director of planning and development for NAFSA: Association of International Educators. In conjunction with her work on NAFSA's Ethics and Self-Study Projects, she has spoken and been published widely on topics related to international student recruitment.

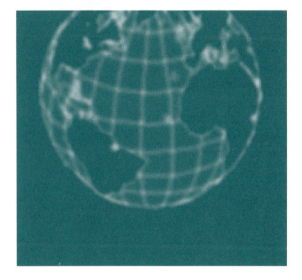

Questions for School Self-Study and Discussion

Note: This exercise can be completed in an afternoon if sufficient data are available and some degree of consensus already exists. Otherwise, a weekend retreat or series of meetings might provide a more realistic time frame. Participants should include the head, one or more trustees, senior faculty, foreign and American students, and representatives from groups both favoring and opposing a change in the foreign student population.

A. Is an international dimension consistent with the school's educational mission? If so, what characteristics does our mission dictate for our international activities?

B. What benefits are anticipated from having more international students? What liabilities might accrue from the change?

- academic
- cultural
- economic
- public relations

How can we be relatively sure of deriving the benefits, while minimizing the liabilities?

C. How many international students should the school have? If a target level is in place, is it consistent with the answers to questions A and B?

D. How diverse should the population be? Should we set specific targets for particular world regions or language groups?

E. What types of students are desired? Do they differ from domestic students?

F. What type of students would be most attracted to our school?

G. What are the school's strengths and weaknesses in terms of the international market? In terms of educating and serving international students?

H. Is the school ready to receive more international students?

- Are the admissions staff/committee equipped?
- How well are we serving the students we have now? Do we meet the standards outlined in the *NAFSA Principles*?
- Should we offer financial aid?
- Should we charge special fees?
- Do we have the advising capacity (academic, personal, immigration)?
- Will we need to conduct special orientation?
- What intercultural programming will we need?
- Will we need to offer ESL?
- How will we provide housing for vacations?
- Are the faculty, staff and students receptive?
- Are the head, trustees, parents and alumni receptive?
- Who will need training in cross-cultural communication?
- Will we need to identify additional international opportunities for faculty development?
- How will we handle college placement for the foreign students?

I. How much of a priority should we make international recruiting?

J. How will we assess our progress?

K. Who needs to know about the school's decision?

Databank

NAIS
PROMOTING
INDEPENDENT
EDUCATION
PROJECT

No. 1, May 1990

BRIEFING

NAIS • PROMOTING INDEPENDENT EDUCATION PROJECT • 75 FEDERAL ST. • BOSTON, MA 02110

What do families unfamiliar with our schools think about independent education?

▼ ▼ ▼

A Report of the Findings from a Series of Focus Group Discussions Sponsored by The Independent Education Fund — NAIS

"The classes are smaller, and they're better at teaching study habits. Sometimes they're more advanced (the course levels), and the classes are smaller so there's more attention."
— *San Francisco Parent*

Following are perceptions about independent education as related to the research firm Belden & Russonello in a series of eight focus groups conducted last year in Atlanta, Denver, San Francisco and Stamford, Connecticut. Belden & Russonello undertook the study under the supervision of the Independent Education Fund (IEF), created by NAIS in 1984 to represent and protect the interests of independent education before Congress, federal agencies and the judiciary.

This information holds value for every NAIS member school. As you read it, you might want to keep the following questions in mind.

■ What preconceived image do 'new market' parents bring to my school?

■ What messages should my school be communicating to address their concerns and correct their misperceptions?

■ How can we reinforce these parents' positive feelings about what we have to offer their children and their community?

■ Are there ways in which we should change our school to better serve those who have no previous experience of independent education—especially families of color?

Who participated in the focus groups?

Nancy Belden and John Russonello put together groups of parents that had the following characteristics: they had children between the ages of 1 and 15; they lived in areas accessible to independent schools; they had incomes equal to the estimated average income of the area's independent school families, and they had no children enrolled in independent schools. African American, White, Asian American and Latino families were represented in the groups.

What does "independent" mean?

■ The terms "independent education" and "independent school" have little meaning to families outside the independent school world. (Some parents guessed that the terms defined an "unstructured educational philosophy," a self study program or home schooling.) "Private school" is an immediately recognizable descriptor, perhaps combined with "independent," as in "private independent school."

What are the positive perceptions of independent schools?

■ Independent schools are somewhat academically superior to local public schools, especially at the secondary level, according to some.

■ Independent schools have tough entrance requirements (though parents doubted that students capable of paying the full tuition would be turned away) according to some.

■ Independent schools have smaller classes and better teachers according to many.

■ Independent schools have newer facilities and better equipment according to some.

■ By the same token, independent schools are perceived by some to have more "special," individualized and extracurricular programs.

■ Some respondents believe independent schools have a more active, involved parent

group.

What about independent school teachers?

■ Independent school teachers are seen by some to be not as qualified as public school teachers, because many have not met public school certification requirements. It is important to note that many members of the public value the oversight functions of public agencies, and do not agree that schools should be free from government regulations.

What are the negative perceptions of independent schools?

■ Independent schools are thought by many to be prohibitively expensive (and most parents underestimated current tuitions of area schools by at least $1,000).

■ The availability of financial aid appears largely unknown. Respondents believe a small percentage of students receives aid (about 15 per cent).

■ Independent schools are thought by many to be "mostly white" with very little racial or socioeconomic diversity.

■ Many respondents believe independent schools are removed from the "real world." Unlike public school students, independent school students are thought to be unhealthily sheltered from reality and diversity.

■ Independent school students are perceived by many to lose connections with, and friendships in, their neighborhood. Parents

would consider independent school, though, if other children from the neighborhood attended the school.

■ Independent schools seem to many respondents to be for "rich kids" or special needs children, unlike public schools, which are for "regular" kids.

How do parents respond to boarding schools?

■ Boarding schools are considered a last resort; although the majority of parents rejected them out of hand, many offered them as a solution to special family circumstances such as traveling, single professional parents, extreme discipline problems, parents working overseas, or parents living in small towns or rural areas where academic options are limited.

What do parents think of the public schools?

■ Many parents are relatively content with public schools, and feel their children are receiving a fair to excellent education there.

■ However, various participants registered the following complaints about public schools:
— They have overcrowded classrooms.
— They don't provide personal attention.
— They don't encourage parental involvement.
— They are unresponsive and uncommunicative.
— Extracurricular offerings are limited by

tax reforms.
— The system favors extremes — the gifted and learning disabled students at the expense of the average children.

Should independent schools exist at all?

■ Most respondents believe that independent schools should continue to exist, because they provide an educational choice for families.

■ Some also suggested independent schools enhance, rather than detract from, public schools because they provide healthy competition.

Who is likely to consider independent schools?

These preliminary data suggest:

■ Those who feel that the public schools system is academically deficient or not good enough for an ambitious parent or child.

■ Those who have a child or children with a special educational need—gifted, learning disabled, possessing a special talent or having some other out of the ordinary need.

■ Those whose son or daughter has a close friend enrolled in an independent school. ❏

NAIS — Promoting Independent Education Project

NAIS has begun a major, multi-year effort to promote independent education and to strengthen the promotion and marketing efforts of individual schools and groups of schools. Through the project, NAIS hopes to:

■ Help member schools collectively to expand their applicant pool, by reaching new and more diverse populations.

■ Promote greater public understanding and appreciation of independent education and to improve its stature and impact especially with respect to:
● parents making educational and financial choices
● legislators and public officials
● those responsible for foundation and corporate giving, *and*
● the leaders of the national education community

Notes

NAIS
PROMOTING
INDEPENDENT
EDUCATION
PROJECT

BRIEFING

No. 2, December 1990

NAIS • PROMOTING INDEPENDENT EDUCATION PROJECT • 75 FEDERAL ST. • BOSTON, MA 02110

What can we learn from market research studies?

▼ ▼ ▼

Results from market research data from independent schools, assembled by NAIS as part of the Promoting Independent Education project, shed new light on marketing opportunities. What some prospective families think about when looking at schools, and how they make choices about educating their children are summarized in this issue of BRIEFING.

Most Important Factors in Choosing a School

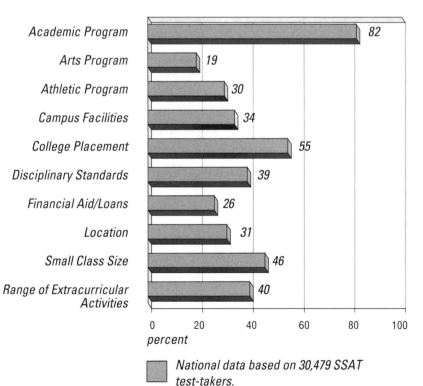

Academic Program	82
Arts Program	19
Athletic Program	30
Campus Facilities	34
College Placement	55
Disciplinary Standards	39
Financial Aid/Loans	26
Location	31
Small Class Size	46
Range of Extracurricular Activities	40

percent

National data based on 30,479 SSAT test-takers.

Misperceptions of independent schools, the lack of understanding and appreciation for the special qualities of independent education, competition from the public schools, and cost represent major marketing and communications challenges. Public perceptions of academic quality, positive educational outcomes, and emphasis on the individual in independent schools constitute excellent opportunities for effective promotion.

This *Briefing* is organized into five sections: the quality of education; community and relationships in independent schools; competition with public schools; cost and affordability; and translating research into marketing strategies.

This *Briefing* covers just some of the findings in the full report, *Summary of Market Research Themes.* To order your copy, see the ordering information on the last page.

Educational quality is foremost in parents' minds

Educational quality is the single most important factor that parents consider in weighing the educational options open to their child. This is true whether parents are considering public, parochial, or independent

- ◆ 76 percent of the parents in one market study cited "quality curriculum" as an important characteristic entering into their decision-making
- ◆ 82 percent of students taking the SSAT (Secondary School Admission Test) listed the strength of the school's academic program as very important in their choice of a school.
- ◆ 70 percent of the students and 62 percent of the parents in one study cited "better education" as the primary factor in their decision.

schools. (On a 5-point scale, "academic quality" rated 4.8 in one research study.) What are other significant considerations to prospective parents?

- ◆ the quality of the faculty
- ◆ the academic standards of the school
- ◆ the concrete outcomes.

The concrete outcomes of the child's educational experience may include admission to college, successful improvement in the child's skills, or overall moral and ethical development.

The six most important school characteristics cited were academic quality, preparation for college, quality of the faculty, close contact with the faculty, emphasis on academic skills, and class size. Three of these findings yield more information offered here.

The importance of quality faculty

A capable, caring and committed faculty is often cited as important in contributing to the reputation of independent schools. A quality faculty is closely linked to academic excellence through the curriculum, the teaching of academic skills and college prepara-

tion. But a capable and stable faculty also contributes to one-to-one interactions with students, mentor relationships, and moral and ethical guidance of students. One school's research showed "the teaching quality of the faculty" to have the highest rating (9.22 out of 10) of any school characteristic. Another school found that the opportunity for close contact with faculty was of greater importance for parents thinking to change from a public to an independent school than it was for parents with children already enrolled in private school.

Small class size emphasized

Small class size and the individual attention that teachers are able to give are seen as strengths of independent schools. When compared with public schools, parents value the benefits of small class size and a tailored curriculum.

From a sample of 177 K-12 independent schools with 92,245 students and 11,193 teachers, there is one teacher for every 8.2 students. At smaller independent schools (300 or less), there is one teacher for every five to six students.

College preparation valued

A school's reputation for academic excellence, which includes the perception of intellectual rigor within a supportive community, has a positive influence on prospective parents. Parents were shown in various studies to see preparation for future schooling and ultimately for college as an important outcome of sending their child to private school. In one market survey, parents were asked to rate specific features and benefits of various school characteristics. Ninety-seven percent of these parents listed "good preparation for college" as either very or extremely important. The only other characteristic that rated high was "academic quality" (99 percent).

The intangible aspects of the educational community and relationships are often overlooked by inquiring families

As with most things, the more you know about them, the more likely you are to discover their many different qualities. So it is with perceptions of what independent schools have to offer. Those least familiar (inquiring parents and students) with independent schools have a sense that they are attended by an exclusive, homogeneous group, and are separate from the "real world." Current parents, students, and alumni on the other hand, describe the school environment as a strong community in which the child develops self-esteem, gains an appreciation of others, and develops meaningful relationships with peers and faculty. These represent markedly different perceptions of the people, process, and purpose of life at an independent school.

The quality of relationships and the dynamics of community are very important for those families enrolled in independent schools. But these intangible aspects of education are often invisible to the general public.

People want to belong to a community. When parents with children in public schools were asked what was important to them,

community and neighborhood ranked high.

The perception exists that enrolling a child in an independent school removes the child from a community. Several significant findings from the research on issues of community and belonging follow:

◆ A supportive, encouraging, family-like environment is seen as an important feature of an independent school to students, alumni, and parents with children currently enrolled. In contrast, to many prospective families, public schools offer a "real world" environment.

◆ The self-empowerment process that happens at many independent schools as a result of small classes, close contact with faculty, and an encouraging environment is understood by families who have direct experience with independent schools. This group sees the opportunities for personal growth and self-realization that can occur as part of the learning process.

◆ All parents place a high value on the school's ability to model and teach moral values and ethical behavior. In the findings of one study, 90 percent of the prospect families felt that it was very important that the school their child attends place importance on high moral standards and stress values.

◆ Meaningful interactions and relationships (with faculty and peers) are viewed as important components of the educational experience according to one study.

◆ Diversity is a strength of independent schools, but not one recognized by prospective families. In fact, in one prospect survey from a day school, 87 percent of the respondents believed that public schools have more diverse student bodies than do either independent or parochial schools. Of the parents with children in public schools interviewed in a prospect study, 51 percent felt that an ethnically and socio-economically diverse student body was very important.

Independent schools should highlight these qualities—community, relationships, moral and ethical behavior, and diversity—to parents and students in their marketing efforts.

There is a high level of general satisfaction with public education—particularly in high-income communities.

Public schools are the chief competitors in the education market

Without question, the biggest competitor to the independent school is the public school. As many as three-quarters of the inquirers at independent schools come from families with children in public schools. Cost puts independent schools at a distinct competitive disadvantage when compared to the perceived-to-be "no cost" public school. What are the perceptions of the competitive positioning between public and independent schools?

◆ There is a high level of general satisfaction with public education—particularly in high-income communities and among families with public school backgrounds. A number of reasons account for a family's allegiance to the public school: cost, convenience, educational value, neighborhood, family tradition, transportation and "real world" issues.

◆ Most families (62 percent) interviewed in one study did not know enough about private education to compare it with education offered in other schools.

◆ There is less satisfaction with the public schools as students move beyond the primary grades. In one survey, 70 percent of parents with children in the 8-10 year-old age bracket were very satisfied with their children's education. That percentage drops to 56 percent for those parents whose children are in the 11-15 year-old category.

◆ Consistent academic quality is seen as an attribute which distinguishes independent schools from public schools. Encouraging creativity and curiosity are also viewed as competitive strengths of independent schools.

◆ Opportunities for creative expression and experience in the arts are perceived to be a strength of the curriculum of an independent school. Independent schools place real emphasis on the creative and performing arts which are often considered "extras" at the public school. In times of state or federal fiscal austerity, it is often these "extras" that are cut from the public school budgets.

How Good a Job is Being Done?
A Comparison of Public, Parochial & Private Schools

Rating	Public	Parochial	Private
Excellent	33.1	7.9	9.4
Good	48.9	24.5	23.7
Fair	13.7	10.1	2.9
Poor	2.2	5.0	1.4
Don't Know	2.2	**52.9**	**62.6**

◆ Structure, discipline and clearly defined codes of behavior are viewed as positive environmental factors at many independent schools. In contrast, public schools are perceived as providing an undisciplined atmosphere for learning by respondents of one survey.

◆ Location and distance from home factor into the decision-making process. Being nearby and offering convenient transportation put the public school at a competitive advantage, particularly in relation to day schools. If transportation were not offered by a day school, 79 percent of the public school parents surveyed said that it would be a problem.

Hours per week spent on various activities, by school type

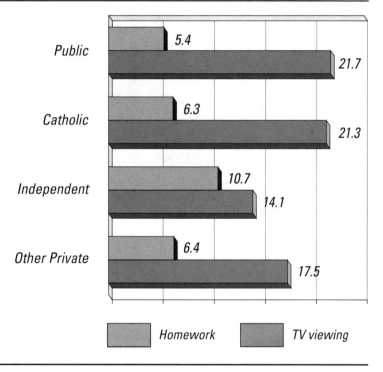

Homework   TV viewing

Source: U.S. Dept. of Education, NCES, NELS:88 Base Year

In another day school survey, more than one-quarter of the families who chose not to apply cited transportation as a significant factor in their decision.

◆ Independent schools are perceived to be less culturally and socio-economically diverse than public schools. Research indicates that prospect families perceive the schools to be exclusive rather than inclusive communities. Eighty-seven percent of the parents interviewed in a prospect survey thought that the public school supported a more diverse student body.

Credits

***Briefing* Advisory Group**
Steve Clem, *Director of Academic Services*

Rick Cowan, *Director of Boarding Schools*

Selby Holmberg, *Director of External Affairs*

Alice Kaufman, *Editor*
Photos: Gabriel A. Cooney

Materials contained in *Briefing* may be reproduced without permission, but please credit NAIS.

Promoting Independent Education

"Promoting Independent Education" is NAIS's multi-year project to promote greater public understanding and appreciation of independent education and to increase the size and diversity of the applicant pool in individual schools. Strategic initiatives to meet these goals focus on the following areas: research, training, public relations, networking and consumer products. This *Briefing* is one of the research initiatives; others include message development, affordability and cost containment, and making use of the National Educational Longitudinal Study. New workshops and publications, press releases, marketing grants to member associations, a consumer directory of NAIS schools, and an independent school brochure are just some of the other initiatives being developed. Future *Briefings* will share new information and strategies for schools.

The expense of an independent education poses a significant marketing challenge

The cost of an independent school education and the lack of awareness of the availability of financial aid limit the ability of many schools to broaden their inquiry and applicant pools.

Who represents the primary market for independent schools?

There are three types of families that can be targeted, each potentially requiring a different marketing approach:

◆ those predisposed toward independent education with the resources to afford it
◆ those who have the resources but need to be assured of its value
◆ those with interest and financial need.

Cost is extremely important to inquiring parents. Survey findings showed that for families whose household income was less than $60,000, tuition and the availability of financial aid ranked in the top 9 considerations in school choice. For families earning

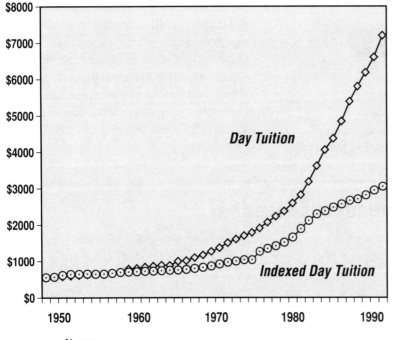

more than $60,000, neither characteristic appeared in the top nine.

Fewer families than ever before can afford an independent education without some financial assistance According to the NAIS Comp* Assist calculation, a 2-parent, 2-child family with assets of $50,000 must have an annual income of $72,000 in order to meet the median 1989-1990 tuition ($13,600) at an independent boarding school. That same family must have an income of approximately $51,000 to meet the median day tuition of $5,987 without financial assistance.

Tuition increases appear to be outpacing many families' ability to pay for an independent education.

Relationship between day tuitions and the consumer price index, 1950-1990

Day Tuition

Indexed Day Tuition

	1950	1960	1970	1980	1990

Notes:
1. Day tuition is a weighted average of 12th grade day tuitions.
2. "Indexed day tuition" is the weighted average of 1954-55 median 12th grade day tuitions, indexed to the CPI-U (1982-84 = 100).

Sources: 1. NAIS Fall Statistics 1981 through 1989. 2. Bureau of Labor Statistics.

How to translate research into marketing strategies

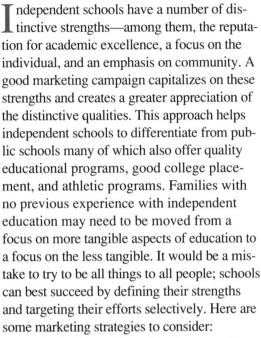

Independent schools have a number of distinctive strengths—among them, the reputation for academic excellence, a focus on the individual, and an emphasis on community. A good marketing campaign capitalizes on these strengths and creates a greater appreciation of the distinctive qualities. This approach helps independent schools to differentiate from public schools many of which also offer quality educational programs, good college placement, and athletic programs. Families with no previous experience with independent education may need to be moved from a focus on more tangible aspects of education to a focus on the less tangible. It would be a mistake to try to be all things to all people; schools can best succeed by defining their strengths and targeting their efforts selectively. Here are some marketing strategies to consider:

♦ Capitalize on the school's reputation for academic quality, rigor, and challenge. Document academic successes, high standards, and excellence in teaching. Don't expect people to take your word for it.

♦ Emphasize academic quality, class size, individual attention, opportunities in the arts, a focus on ethics, attention to moral values, diversity, community, access, facilities, successful educational outcomes, and a "safe" environment.

♦ Be an advocate and a cheerleader for those aspects of your school's culture that value academic and artistic achievement. Spotlight faculty—their credentials, innovative teaching techniques, commitment and positive relationships with students.

♦ Use parents, faculty, and students to communicate with inquiring families. In catalogues and brochures use quotes and photographs to convey your message.

Community, relationships and atmosphere are crucial dimensions

Creating an attractive school catalogue to send to inquiring parents and students may be the *first* step in arousing interest, but personal contact remains the most effective marketing tool and the most underutilized. Use your faculty in the visiting and interviewing process and target both parents and children, because

they are both involved in the final decision.

♦ Document relationships—friendships and interactions between students and faculty, students with one another, students and alumni.

♦ Take full advantage of contacts with students, faculty and head during on-campus visits to paint a friendly picture of the school's community and culture. Use pictures and testimonials in school promotionals to show "atmosphere," school spirit, friendships, and a sense of community and belonging.

♦ Create positive first impressions, whether in catalogues or personal contacts. Focus on the less visible qualities of the school: developing self-esteem, and emphasis on moral and ethical values.

♦ Broaden visibility through on-campus events, community events, and direct mail. Develop cooperative programs with local public schools. Take every opportunity to get "in the news."

♦ Make the most of the campus visit with signage, tours, class visits, interviews. Encourage all-day and/or overnight stays.

Making the case for affordability

The cost of an independent education is a major consideration for families considering private school. How a school communicates affordability is important. Here are some specific suggestions for overcoming the cost and affordability hurdle:

♦ Define and present specific educational outcomes of value—identifying tangible and intangible benefits of an independent education.

♦ Highlight financial aid programs and services early and often in marketing literature and in correspondence to inquiring families. Provide statistical information about financial aid funds and average awards as well as financial profiles of currently enrolled families receiving assistance.

♦ Consider a financing/affordability brochure to send to all inquiring families.

♦ Conduct financial aid and financial planning workshops for prospective families.

♦ Consider alternative payment plans, creative financing options, the possibility of tuition discounts, and institutional loan programs.

Notes

NAIS
PROMOTING
INDEPENDENT
EDUCATION
PROJECT

No. 3, March 1991

BRIEFING

NATIONAL ASSOCIATION OF INDEPENDENT SCHOOLS • BOSTON, MASSACHUSETTS • WASHINGTON, D.C.

What's on the minds of parents who don't choose independent schools?

▼ ▼ ▼

*A report on in-depth interviews conducted for the
NAIS Independent Education Fund*

Having high quality teachers is the number one criterion parents choose (from a list of 10) in evaluating both high schools and elementary schools...followed by small class sizes, opportunities for parental involvement, and a friendly social environment for students.

The first issue of *Briefing* published last May reported on a series of eight focus groups conducted in four U.S. cities with parents of school-age children. The families had incomes equal to independent school families in their area, and had considered but had not enrolled their children in independent schools.

Among those focus group participants were a significant number of parents who were clearly sympathetic to independent schools. To find out what could motivate those parents to enroll their sons and daughters in independent schools, NAIS and the Independent Education Fund (IEF) commissioned the Washington firm of Belden & Russonello to conduct a follow-up survey. This issue of *Briefing* presents a summary of 28 in-depth interviews with those parents.

Who was interviewed for this research?

Parents selected for the follow-up study were chosen because they seemed reasonably sympathetic to independent education. IEF reviewed videotapes from the original eight focus group discussions in making their selections for this study. Represented among the 41 people chosen were a balance of men and women from different racial backgrounds with yearly income levels ranging from $25,000 to $200,000.

Letters explaining this research project and asking for their participation were sent to each of the 41 parents, and in follow-up phone calls, 28 agreed to be interviewed. Appointments were made for the lengthy phone interviews at times convenient for the cooperating parents.

How was the study conducted?

Interviews were conducted using a carefully constructed two-part questionnaire. The first section addressed parents' opinions about particular positive and negative qualities of independent and public schools at all grade levels; the second section focussed on eight message statements, each of which highlights a positive attribute of an independent school education.

The interviews took, on average, 35 minutes to administer. During the interview, parents were asked to open an envelope which they had received in the mail marked "Do Not Open Until the Interviewer Calls You." It contained eight flash cards in random order, each with a single message statement related to independent schools. The

are white collar professional (e.g., attorney, engineer, stockbroker). Six of the households are white collar sales or technical, two are white collar clerical, and only one household is blue collar.

Most (15) of the households are two income families. Twelve have only one spouse working, and one parent said that he and his wife only work part-time.

Highlights of Findings

What could move these parents to enroll their children in an independent school?

■ if the public schools deteriorate,

■ if their children develop special needs that the public schools cannot address, or

■ if they had more money to afford an independent school.

What message would motivate parents to consider independent schools, regardless of financial or public school considerations?

■ First, if they are convinced that an independent school will give their child an academic advantage to get into an outstanding college.

■ Second, if an independent school gives their child individual attention, even if the child is just an average student.

■ Third, if an independent school helps to build character and instill values in students.

What other messages also motivate some parents to consider independent schools?

■ The lack of bureaucracy in independent schools gives them the freedom to choose the best teachers and to keep only those teachers who measure up.

■ Independent schools make a point of involving parents in the education of their children.

What factors may not be as decisive or influential in making the independent school decision?

While parents place importance on schools ensuring that every student has the opportunity to work together with students of other ethnic backgrounds and to participate in arts, music and sports programs, these attributes may not be decisive or influential factors when these parents consider a school.

parents were asked to open the envelope, read the messages, and rank them according to how important each was to them in considering schools for their children.

What was the profile of families who participated?

The majority (17) of the parents interviewed have two children. Six have three children, two have four children, two have one child, and one parent has five children.

The majority (16) of families have at least one child in elementary school. Six families have at least one child in middle school, four families have at least one child in high school, and two families have a child in pre-school or day care.

Most of the parents interviewed (19) have considered sending their children to an independent school. When asked, these parents offered the names of eight NAIS-member schools as previously under consideration. Several parents either could not remember specific school names, had not thought about particular schools, or offered the names of parochial or non-NAIS military schools.

The majority (22) of these parents attended public elementary and high school themselves. Four others attended parochial schools, and two parents attended private, independent high schools. When asked about their own educational experience, all parents said they were either "very satisfied" (21) or "somewhat satisfied" (seven).

The households represented by these parents are predominantly white collar managerial (11 households). Eight of the households

Demographic Composition of Respondents	
All	**28**
Sex	
Female	14
Male	14
Marital	
Married	27
Divorced	1
Race	
White	15
Black	8
Hispanic	4
Asian	1
Cities	
Atlanta	10
Denver	8
San Francisco	4
Stamford	6
Household	
Professional white-collar	8
White-collar managerial	11
White-collar sales/technical	6
White-collar clerical	2
Blue-collar	1
Total Household Income*	
$25,000-$30,000	4
$30,000-$40,000	1
$40,000+	8
$50,000+	4
$75,000-$100,000	2
$100,000-$150,000	8
$150,000-$200,000	1

Income categories used to recruit participants varied in each city and were based on the estimated average household income of parents whose children currently attend area independent schools.

What are some perceptions about the independent school community?

■ Most parents do not believe that independent schools stress participation and teamwork over winning in sports; nor do they believe that students at a small independent school are more likely than those in public schools to work together with students of other racial and ethnic backgrounds.

■ Parents prefer co-educational over single-sex schools at the elementary as well as high school levels.

■ Parents tend to view independent schools as elitist, but this elitism would not make an independent school unacceptable to most. Other attributes of independent schools, such as the individual attention and academic training, are more important considerations for these parents.

Eight Messages Tested in Interviews with Public School Parents

✎ Independent schools give students an academic advantage to get into an outstanding college.

✎ Children in independent schools do not have to be at the top or the bottom of the class to receive special attention. Independent schools treat every student as special, helping each child to discover his or her own talents and do his or her best.

✎ The lack of bureaucracy in independent schools gives them the freedom to choose the best, most caring teachers, and the freedom to keep only those teachers who measure up.

✎ Independent schools make a point of involving parents with their child's education; parents have extensive, ongoing communication with teachers at independent schools.

✎ Building character and integrity is just as important as academic achievement at independent schools. By addressing values, independent schools help students develop their ability to reason and to make choices about how they will live.

✎ In independent schools, participation in the arts and music are an integral part of every student's education.

✎ Unlike in many public schools, students in small independent schools work together and socialize with students of other ethnic and racial backgrounds.

✎ Sports at independent schools stress participation and teamwork over simply winning.

Where do teachers and class size fit into the decision process?

Having high quality teachers is the number one criterion parents chose (from a list of 10) in evaluating both high schools and elementary schools. Teacher quality is followed by small class sizes, opportunities for parental involvement, and a friendly social environment for students.

Parents who have previously considered independent schools for their children did so because they were looking for smaller class sizes, more individual attention for their children, higher quality teachers, or more discipline in the school environment. These same parents ultimately decided to use or stay in the public schools for two primary reasons: general satisfaction with their public schools and the high cost of independent schools.

How are issues of cost and affordability perceived by these parents?

Parents worry that college is very costly, but they see it as a *necessary* expense of their children's education; parents tend to view private elementary, middle school, and high school education as a very costly but *optional* expense. Therefore, college has first priority for their funds.

If parents were going to send their children to an independent school, they would be more likely to want to pay for it from their savings than borrow from relatives or a bank.

The research confirms a diversity of attitudes.

The primary purpose of conducting the interviews was to further explore what messages, if any, could move select public school parents to enroll their children in an independent school. The results of these interviews cannot be construed as reliably representing a national sample. However, these interviews do shed light on the diversity of attitudes toward key messages and provide insight into which messages have the potential for changing behavior.

Using the results of these interviews as a guide, the Independent Education Fund has commissioned a much larger, national poll to provide quantitative research on key messages for the use of NAIS member schools. The conclusions of the national research will be reported as soon as they are available.

Notes

NAIS
PROMOTING
INDEPENDENT
EDUCATION
PROJECT

No. 4, May 1991

BRIEFING

NATIONAL ASSOCIATION OF INDEPENDENT SCHOOLS • BOSTON, MASSACHUSETTS • WASHINGTON, D.C.

Pricing and Affordability

▼ ▼ ▼

This Briefing reports on some of the highlights of a longer paper on pricing and affordability prepared by Peter Aitken, NAIS director of research and information services (See form on last page to order the full report). These highlights include: background data on demographics and family income; the relationship between independent school tuitions, the consumer price index and broader measures of the ability of families to pay for independent education; consideration of the role of financial aid in enhancing access to independent schools; and an "independent school affordability index," analogous to the "housing affordability index." NAIS respects the autonomy of individual schools with regard to mission and operations, has no prescriptive role here, and seeks none. The project on pricing and affordability will offer resources that complement and support the planning work of individual schools in unusually complicated times. Please note that while footnotes are not given in this Briefing, the original paper provides detailed references for all of the data presented here.

Introduction

Just as crosscurrents in a river cause turbulence, conflicting influences upon independent education at this time are making for a bumpy ride. Six interrelated factors contribute to the disequilibrium for schools. Three of these are directly related to common policy goals. The fourth is pricing, itself largely a consequence of policy goals. The fifth and sixth are environmental factors. The six factors are:

- **Access:** a general commitment on the part of schools to increase socioeconomic participation in independent education.
- **Financial aid:** the most significant strategy adopted by schools in their efforts to increase socioeconomic diversity in enrollments.

This report explores relationships between independent schools and the U. S. population at large, particularly with regard to the ability to pay tuitions.

- **Faculty compensation:** efforts by many schools to achieve substantial increases in teachers' salaries.
- **Pricing:** an extended trend in tuition and fee increases exceeding the rates of growth of the consumer price index and other measures of people's ability to pay for independent education.
- **Demographics:** the impact of the "baby bust" and the projected impact of the "baby boomlet" on school enrollments.
- **Recession:** a family's decision to choose independent schooling is vulnerable to a downturn in its financial circumstances.

Because expanding access to independent schools is one of the fundamental issues underlying this inquiry, this report explores relationships between independent schools and the U. S. population at large, particularly with regard to the ability to pay tuitions. Data on demographics and income are crucial to an understanding of the challenges schools face.

Demographics

First, it is important to understand the essential characteristics of the demographic roller coaster that is partly responsible for our bumpy ride.

- The "baby boomers," born between 1945 and 1965 represent approximately one third of total U.S. population. Now aged between 26 and 46, they contribute significantly to the aging of the population, and they are moving beyond their childbearing years.

- The "baby bust," those born between 1965 and 1976, represent one fifth of total U. S. population. Aged between 15 and 26, they are moving into their family-making and childbearing years.

- Born since 1976, the "baby boomlet," a smaller group than the original "baby boom," may be a less well understood demographic phenomenon. According to Harold Hodgkinson, "the Baby Boomlet kids now coming through our elementary schools are *not* [primarily] children of the Boom but children of minorities. From 1985 to 2000, the nation's youth population will increase by 2.4 million Hispanics, 1.7 million blacks, 483,000 other ethnic children, and 60,000 Caucasians."

Projections such as these are based on three factors: the existing age distribution of racial and ethnic groups within the population, differential birth rates, and immigration. Hodgkinson points out that birth rates (children per female) are 1.7 for whites, 2.1 for Puerto Ricans, 2.4 for blacks, and 2.9 for Mexican Americans. A birth rate of about 2.1 children per female sustains a steady population. Compounding the effect of these differential birth rates on population projections, Hodgkinson notes that the average white in the United States in 1985 was 31 years old, the average black 25, and the average Hispanic 22. Thus the typical Hispanic female was at the beginning of her childbearing years, while the average white female was nearing the end of hers.

Evidence of the impact of these demographic changes is already apparent in public elementary and secondary schools. By 1985, public elementary schools in California already enrolled a "majority of minorities." At the same time, minorities represented 46% of enrollment in Texas public schools; half of all states had public school enrollments including more than 25% minorities; and all 25 of the largest urban public school systems had "majority minority" enrollments.

Family Incomes and Household Net Worth

The *median income* of all U. S. families in 1988 was $32,191. The median incomes of white, black, and Hispanic-origin families in 1988 were respectively $33,915, $19,329, and $21,769. *Incomes of the most affluent* (i.e., the top fifth, by income) white and black families in 1987 were respectively above $54,280 and above $36,652.

The *average after-tax income* of American households in 1986 was $23,683. The corresponding figures for white, black, and Hispanic-origin households were $24,570, $16,398, and $18,817.

In 1987, the *average annual discretionary expenditure* (i.e., for items other than food, housing, clothes, transportation, health care, pensions, social security, and taxes) *of husband and wife families* with an oldest child between the ages of 6 and 17, was $5,143.

The *median net worth of American households* in 1988 was about $36,000. The median net worth of white, black, and Hispanic-origin households in 1988 was respectively $43,279, $4,169, and $5,524. *Median net worth of the most affluent* (i.e., the top fifth in terms of income) white, black, and Hispanic-origin households in 1988 was respectively $119,057, $47,160, and $58,731.

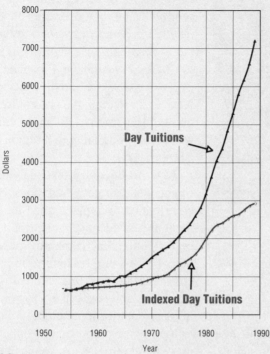

A. NAIS Member Day School Tuitions (12th Grade) 1950 to 1990

Day Tuitions

Indexed Day Tuitions

Source: NAIS Statistics

Note: Up to and including 1987-88, the chart shows the weighted average of 12th grade day tuitions for various sub-groups of schools comprising all day schools. After 1987-88, it shows median tuitions for all day schools as a single group.

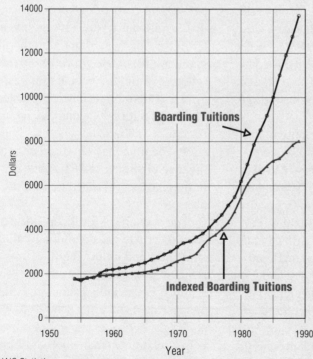

B. NAIS Member Boarding School Tuitions (12th Grade) 1950 to 1990

Boarding Tuitions

Indexed Boarding Tuitions

Source: NAIS Statistics

Note: Up to and including 1987-88, the chart shows the weighted average of boarding tuitions for various sub-groups of schools comprising all boarding schools. After 1987-88, it shows median tuitions for all boarding schools as a single group.

Independent School Tuitions and the Consumer Price Index

Day and boarding school tuitions have far outpaced the consumer price index, especially since 1980 (see charts A and B). The upper line on each chart is the actual median 12th grade NAIS tuition. The lower line on each chart, called "indexed tuition," shows what the tuitions would have been had they been indexed, or locked, to the consumer price index (CPI) beginning in 1954-55. Until the early 1980s, boarding school tuitions closely paralleled the CPI. Day tuitions crept ahead, though not dramatically, beginning in the 1960s. By contrast with these long-term trends, tuitions in both day and boarding schools have risen much faster than the CPI since the early 1980s.

The rapid rise of tuitions since the early 1980s is almost certainly related to schools' increased commitment to faculty salaries in this period. From 1950 to about 1970, salaries grew a little faster than the CPI. From 1970 to 1980, the reverse was true. The median salary gained about $2,750, or 25%, in 1980 dollars, over the 30-year period from 1950 to 1980, against the CPI. Since 1980, it has been a different story. In ten years, the median salary has gained about $7,250, or about 40%, in 1990 dollars, against the CPI.

From the figures on tuitions and family incomes, one conclusion stands out immediately. As a proportion of median household income, day tuitions range from about 20% for white families to about 40% for black families, and this relationship worsened during the 1980s. By this measure, independent schools were becoming less affordable.

Now, if we assume that tuitions are generally paid from *after-tax, discretionary income*, they are even less affordable for most families. In fact, the 1986-87 and 1987-88 median 12th grade day tuitions ($5,800 and $6,180) exceeded the *average total discretionary expenditure* for husband and wife households with an oldest child between 6 and 17 ($5,143) in 1987. It was only for the top fifth of households (by income) that discretionary expenditures (about $8,000) could even *theoretically* encompass a 12th grade median day tuition (about $6,000). And if a family had two children, or modest expenses beyond the essentials of food, housing, clothes, health care, etc., independent school

recent trends in its deployment raise some serious policy questions. A ten-year, 260% increase in total financial aid dollars, to the current level of $267 million per year, representing 8% of total operating expense, has resulted in a mere *12% increase in the number of financial aid recipients as a percentage of total enrollment.* Financial aid is an expensive way to build diversity in our schools. Projecting the present trends is highly discouraging. Financial aid policy seems to be operating in a region of diminishing returns.

In terms of education and equity, present financial aid strategy makes a substantial contribution to implementing the goals of many independent schools. But it is far from perfect and, in fact, embodies some potentially serious mid- to long-term problems. In cost-benefit terms, financial aid is extremely expensive and is not likely to be sustainable in its present form indefinitely. Furthermore, as long as the proportion of students on financial aid remains low, typically less than one fifth of school enrollments, the strategy of charging high tuitions and redistributing dollars via financial aid sustains a "noblesse oblige" conception of the independent school.

There may be solutions to this dilemma.

◆ There is a strong case for reducing the per student costs of independent schools so that significantly (say 25% or 35%) lower tuitions result in substantial, rather than marginal, improvements in access to independent schools by middle income families.

◆ Creative financing, represented in a variety of tuition loan and payment plans, should be encouraged wherever appropriate.

◆ The time may have come to reexamine the idea of sliding scale tuitions–variable tuition payments related to families' ability to pay.

The way ahead for independent schools should include consideration of all these strategies, and more. The fundamental goal remains to expand access to independent schools. Financial aid should continue to have a role in enabling schools to reach out across the entire socioeconomic spectrum to help a relatively small number of families who would not otherwise be able to send their children to independent schools.

educations were clearly beyond reach, even for the average family in this top income quintile.

Financial Aid

Independent schools are autonomous, free market institutions. They have traditionally believed in low student:teacher ratios, strong academic and extracurricular programs, small school size, excellent facilities, and the development of the whole child. But these commitments are expensive. The 1988-89 average cost per student in NAIS schools, $8,716, was double the estimated figure of $4,348 for public schools. The more nearly comparable figure of $7,328 for NAIS elementary/secondary day schools is still nearly 70% higher than the public school per student cost. The pricing of independent schools narrows their market, and defines the kinds of institutions they are.

Financial aid is a central strategy in the efforts of independent schools to broaden socioeconomic access and diversify their enrollments. In 1989-90, 800 NAIS member schools awarded $267 million in financial aid to nearly 60,000 students representing 18% of total enrollment. About one fifth of total financial aid went to faculty and staff children, and these children comprised about one fifth of the total number of financial aid recipients. On the face of it, at 8% of total operating expenses, financial aid represents a major commitment by independent schools.

But the news is not all good. Financial aid exists to increase the socioeconomic diversity of independent school enrollments; yet

In terms of education and equity, present financial aid strategy makes a substantial contribution to implementing the goals of many independent schools. But it is far from perfect and, in fact, embodies some potentially serious mid- to long-term problems.

The Independent School Affordability Index

Defining affordability

The first step in developing an independent school affordability index is to decide on a definition of "affordability."

The NAIS School and Student Service for Financial Aid (SSS) uses a sophisticated methodology for estimating how much a family can afford to contribute to the educational expenses of a child attending an independent school. The SSS calculation takes into consideration a number of criteria, including family income and net worth, parents' age, whether one or two parents are earning, the number of children attending tuition-charging institutions, etc. A school then uses this information, in conjunction with its own tuition, to compute an appropriate financial aid award.

To gauge the affordability of a school, we use the SSS calculation in reverse. Among the inputs, we supply the figure for the family's contribution to educational expenses for its child, setting this equal to the school's tuition. In this way, we have defined the family that can *just afford* the tuition. Other inputs must include relevant data about the

family's financial position. If we supply average or median figures for U. S. families, then the reverse SSS calculation can be made to yield the one key item of data that we do not provide, family income. Then, because initially we set the family's contribution to educational expenses just equal to the school's tuition, the family income we calculate is the income that makes the school just affordable.

To generalize with regard to schools, we use 12th grade day and boarding tuitions. To generalize with regard to families, we use national median figures for net worth. Our reverse SSS calculation also assumes the following family characteristics: a married couple family with both partners earning, the older parent aged 38, two children under the age of 18, both attending tuition-charging institutions.

Using these characteristics, the reverse SSS calculation yields *the threshold income level at which the typical or most common kind of family can just afford independent school tuitions.*

Creating the independent school affordability index

The next step is to locate this threshold income on a chart showing the distribution of U. S. family incomes. Chart C shows the distribution of after-tax household incomes in 1987. Threshold income levels for affording day and boarding tuitions *for two children* are indicated. These are about $45,000 and $60,000 respectively. Chart D is very similar, but across the bottom it shows the cumulative percentage of households with incomes below the indicated dollar levels. So, we can deduce the percentage of U. S. households that have incomes above the threshold levels and who are therefore able to afford independent school tuitions *for two children*, according to SSS criteria and methodology. *This percentage becomes the "independent school affordability index."*

The affordability index for day and boarding schools

The index (see Chart E) for day schools is about 12% (i.e., 88% of households fall below the threshold income level), and for boarding schools about 4% (96% of households fall below the threshold income level). Quite simply these are the percentages of

C. Distribution of After-Tax Household Incomes (1987)

Married Couple Families with Related Children

Day Affordability Threshold

Boarding Affordability Threshold

Income Range ($000's)

Source: U.S. Department of Commerce, Bureau of the Census Current Population Reports; Special Studies, Series P-23, No. 126

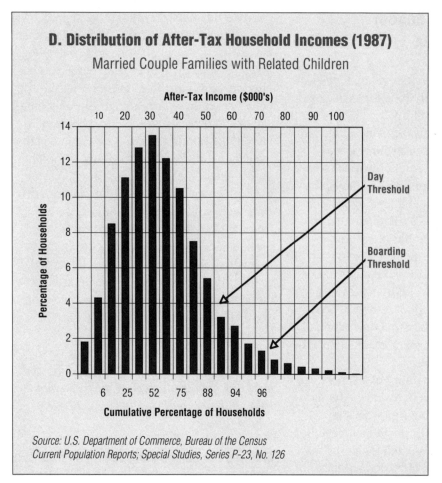

D. Distribution of After-Tax Household Incomes (1987)

Married Couple Families with Related Children

After-Tax Income ($000's)

Day Threshold

Boarding Threshold

Cumulative Percentage of Households

Source: U.S. Department of Commerce, Bureau of the Census
Current Population Reports; Special Studies, Series P-23, No. 126

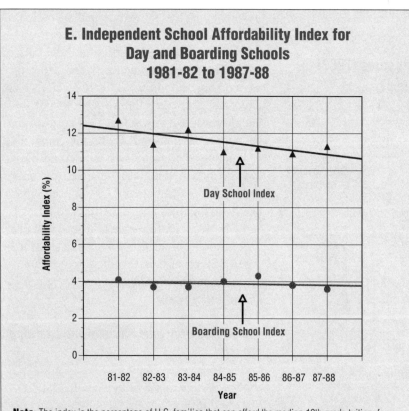

E. Independent School Affordability Index for Day and Boarding Schools 1981-82 to 1987-88

Day School Index

Boarding School Index

Year

Note: The index is the percentage of U.S. families that can afford the median 12th grade tuition, for two children.

Main assumptions: two parents both earning, older parent aged 38, family net worth equivalent to the median for U.S. families, two children attending tuition charging institutions.

families that are able to afford independent schools for their children, based on the assumptions and methodology described above. The independent school affordability index, as defined here, has been calculated for selected years in the 1980s. Indexes for both day and boarding tuitions are shown in Chart E. It is, of course, no surprise that these indexes confirm that only a small proportion of American families can afford independent schools. What is more disturbing, especially in the case of day schools, is that *we are becoming less affordable.*

What can be done to reverse the trend of decreasing affordability?

We need to find a way to conduct a dialogue about aspects of characteristic independent school mission, program, and financial structure that have the potential to yield large changes in per student costs.

What is meant by "large changes in per student costs?"

The answer is something that goes beyond improved financial management, more aggressive fund-raising, and stoic belt-tightening. These are familiar paths that we have all traveled. Our efforts have played a part in *containing tuition increases* while we have simultaneously achieved real improvements in faculty salaries. But large changes in per student costs mean changes that lead to significant *reductions in tuition.* While an 11% reduction in tuition would marginally help the upper middle income class, we need to aim at something closer to 25%. Certainly, we have to move way beyond annual heroics with the budget, enabling us to hold down next year's tuition increase to 7% instead of 9%. We must undertake a fundamental reexamination of traditional assumptions about school mission and structure, curriculum, teaching, learning, and the needs and interests of faculties, families, and children, all with the aim of identifying viable models of a new and leaner kind of independent school. This is an ambitious research agenda.

Next Steps: the Research Agenda
What will the research team address?

The NAIS Project on Pricing and Affordability is seeking foundation support to sponsor a research team to undertake a task that resembles strategic planning for a hypothetical school. In developing a variety of possible models or scenarios, the team can fearlessly question cherished traditional assumptions and articles of faith and explore the potential of new structures and approaches.

It is clear that, early on in this endeavor, issues such as student/teacher ratio, curriculum, extracurricular programs, faculty and administrative structure, teachers' career patterns, school organization, length of school year, use of plant and facilities, and economies of scale in inter-school collaborations will arise. In fact, the work will almost certainly begin with some soul-searching about how much schools should attempt to undertake in educating children.

NAIS Project on Pricing and Affordability

Begun in early 1990, the NAIS Project on Pricing and Affordability has three goals. The first is to study and document the relationship between independent school tuitions and the consumer price index and broader measures of the ability of families to pay for independent education. This goal also includes consideration of the role of financial aid in enhancing access to independent schools.

The second goal of the project is to develop an "independent school affordability index." This index is somewhat analogous to the "housing affordability index" that relates housing prices to family incomes through an easily understood numerical measure of access to financing for house purchase. The independent school affordability index will be used to monitor the relationship between tuitions and the ability of families to pay for independent education for their children, serving as an indicator of progress toward or away from the goal of broader socioeconomic access to independent schools.

These first two goals have been reached and this *Briefing* highlights the results.

The third goal is to undertake research into those aspects of independent school financial structure and operations with the greatest potential to yield reductions in cost per student. NAIS hopes to develop a variety of alternative models or scenarios, offering avenues to reduced per student costs, that may be useful to schools as they do their own planning. Studies will be undertaken, over a two year period, by a research team including trustees, school heads, financial officers, economists, and others. Reports will be made in conference presentations and published as working papers. NAIS is pursuing foundation support for this research.

Could less be more?

Doing less in schools is usually harder than doing more. Any program in any school at any given time represents the results of the energy and commitment of a number of people, often over many years. We do not lightly abandon these investments, and, in fact, our belief in education and our commitment to strengthening our schools usually find us eager to undertake new initiatives. But if, over a long period of time, we are better at adding new programs than at closing old ones down, we run the risk of eroding almost everything we believe in. Quantity crowds out quality. Fundamental goals are sacrificed, victims to accumulated pressures for more, and ever fancier versions of everything from five-star dormitories and major-league athletic facilities to luxurious advanced courses enrolling three students. The remedy lies in deciding what is really important to do well, and in knowing when and how to stop doing a large number of things only moderately well in order to do a smaller number really well.

Acknowledgements

Contributors to the research and analysis reported in this paper included Gloria Berenson, SSS Program Director at Educational Testing Service, Princeton, N.J.; Elizabeth Alling, Associate Director of Development at the Lawrence Academy at Groton, MA; John Reydel, Jr., a master's degree candidate at the Harvard Graduate School of Education; Matthew Chiccuarelli, Manager of Data Operations, and Martha Westburg, Assistant for Special Projects in the department of Research and Information Services at NAIS.

Notes